To Evelyn

Best wishes

Meurs Lewnsbau

Parliamentary Pioneers

Photograph opposite: Labour women MPs elected in 1929 outside the Houses of Parliament - Lady Cynthia Mosley, Dr Marion Phillips, Susan Lawrence, Edith Picton-Turbervill, Margaret Bondfield, Dr Ethel Bentham, Ellen Wilkinson, Mary Hamilton and Jenny Lee

Parliamentary Pioneers

LABOUR WOMEN MPs
1918 – 1945

Mary Honeyball

Publications

First published in Great Britain in 2015
by Urbane Publications Ltd
Suite 3, Brown Europe House, 33/34 Gleamingwood Drive,
Chatham, Kent ME5 8RZ
Copyright © Mary Honeyball, 2015

A CIP catalogue record for this book is available
from the British Library.

ISBN 978-1-909273-85-6
EPUB 978-1-909273-86-3

Design and Typeset by The Invisible Man

Printed and bound by CPI Group (UK) Ltd, Croydon, CR0 4YY

Urbanepubliations.com

The publisher supports the Forest Stewardship Council® (FSC®), the leading
international forest-certification organisation. This book is made from acid-free
paper from an FSC®-certified provider. FSC is the only forest-certification scheme
supported by the leading environmental organisations, including Greenpeace.

In memory of Chris Underwood

for your love and inspiration

.

Testimonials

Rt Hon Dame Margaret Beckett DBE MP,

former Leader of the Labour Party and Foreign Secretary:

Parliamentary Pioneers tells the story of an intrinsic piece of Labour history and it is surprising that it has not yet been told. We learn how tough it was for those first Labour women, perhaps it was so hard that some women were put off completely. But the modern trailblazers who Mary features in this book show how life for Labour women has improved not least because there is mutual respect between Labour men and women but also, as Honeyball's book suggests, there is parity which has only been achieved because Labour women fought hard to get it. It's been a remarkable journey and I'm so pleased this account has been recorded so well.

Rt Hon Charles Clarke,

former Home Secretary and author of *The Too Difficult Box*:

Parliamentary Pioneers charts a period of history that is not only rarely covered in mainstream debate but it gives us insight into the struggle women politicians endured, and the alienation they were often met with from some colleagues within the very male dominated environment of Westminster. It explores the opportunities they created for themselves to thrive during political debate and while making new policies. *Parliamentary Pioneers* eloquently draws our attention to the fight these doughty early pioneers fearlessly took on and brings the discussion into the 21st century by asking two formidable current Labour women MPs to share their experiences.

Baroness Joyce Gould of Potternewton,
former Labour Party Chief Woman Officer and National Agent:

At a period when women are still so underrepresented in British politics Mary couldn't have chosen a more prescient time to publish *Parliamentary Pioneers*. This is an important reminder not only of the early struggle following the suffragette movement, but of how these tough women worked so hard to dismantle entrenched views on gender and risked being ridiculed in the process. It was a difficult time but it undoubtedly helped to encourage future generations of women to stand for Parliament and to become politically active. We have yet to reach a critical mass of gender representation in British politics, and Mary's book explains why that journey has been, and continues to be, so hard.

Glenis Willmott MEP,
Labour MEP for the East Midlands and leader of the European Parliamentary Labour Party:

Parliamentary Pioneers superbly explores the humble beginnings of the Labour women's movement and their rise to parliamentary politics. The journey for recognition and better representation has been tumultuous at times, as Mary's book finely displays. Despite the fact we still have some way to go the Labour Party has made significant strides since the day in 1924 when the first Labour women were elected. While in Europe there is greater gender balance, Mary's book reveals through interviews with two leading Labour women that we are very much still on that journey to full parity in the UK.

Rowena Mason,

Political Correspondent for The Guardian:

Parliamentary Pioneers covers a fascinating period of political history after the suffragette movement when some of the first women to enter parliament were not even able to vote for themselves to be there. Honeyball fills a gap in the knowledge of many of us by exploring the careers of trailblazing female Labour MPs who were among the first to break into the male-dominated environment of Westminster.

Acknowledgements

This book has been a long time in the making. Now it is finally wending its way to the stores, the shelves and the internet, I wish to thank those who made the whole thing possible.

Firstly are the trio of Rebecca Vagg, Kate Brooks and Ruby Thompson who provided invaluable help and support and who all were an integral part of the book's creation and production. My sincere thanks to all three of you.

My thanks too to Sarah Mackinlay who was there at all the crucial moments sorting things out and promoting the book in her own inimitable way. Thank you Sarah for your faith in both this project and in me as a first time author.

I must also mention Mark Nottingham who was always there and made sure I found the time to put the book together.

Last but not least among the main characters is Matthew Smith of Urbane Publications. Matthew took this book on knowing little about either me or my credentials. I just hope his confidence is rewarded.

Special recognition is also due to the People's History Museum in Manchester who were extremely helpful in finding research material for the book and coming up with many of the images you will find on these pages.

My sincere thanks to Rt Honourable Harriet Harman QC MP and Stella Creasy MP, for contributing to the concluding chapter. Their sharp insights illustrate just how far there is still to go to ensure true equality between women and men in the British Parliament.

Contents

Introduction

There has been surprisingly little written about the first female Members of Parliament, elected following women gaining the vote in 1918. As someone with personal experience of being a woman in the Labour Party, I want to share the lives and experiences of my predecessors with you, those pioneers who made it possible for me to be in my role today. While it would be easy to write many deserved books on Labour women MPs and their successes over the past 80 years, this book specifically concentrates on the period 1918 to 1945, the end of the First World War to the end of the Second.

> "The Labour Party is the Women's Party. Woman is the Chancellor of the Exchequer of the home."

The 1918 Labour Party general election manifesto gave the official view, the 'party' line: women were homemakers, their role domestic, their concerns revolving around husband and family. However, the Labour Party was only articulating the social reality of the time, namely that working-class women had little choice other than to seek male protection in marriage. The single lifestyle in the 1920s and 30s, while perhaps an option for the rich, required a very brave spirit indeed if a woman was not so prosperous.

The first full chapter in this book looks at the campaign for birth control, a concern high on the list of issues for women members of the Labour Party. The cause was supported, though not particularly effectively championed, by some of the first Labour women MPs. The attempt to gain the means to limit family size demonstrates the tensions between the priorities of the Labour Party leadership and the concerns of its women members. As such it provides a vivid picture of the position of the first Labour women MPs within the Party.

The subsequent four chapters explore areas where the first Labour women MPs played a significant role in developing policy, their experiences in the House of Commons, and their relationship with the Labour Party. Following the first chapter on birth control, each subsequent chapter will start with a short account of the MPs who were most prominent within each area, and then explore the issues in more depth.

- **Work**: Margaret Bondfield was the champion of the working woman and this chapter explores her efforts to improve the working life of women both before and after she entered the House of Commons. It also examines the work-related matters women MPs championed both in Parliament and throughout the country, including their involvement in the General Strike and the effects of the Great Depression and mass unemployment.

- **Welfare**: Three of the early Labour women MPs were active in this area - Susan Lawrence who became Parliamentary Secretary to the Ministry of Health in 1929; Edith Summerskill, a doctor in general practice who was elected to Parliament in 1938; and the Labour Party Chief Woman Officer, Marion Phillips, who served as an MP for a short time in 1931. As MPs all three were pivotal in campaigns to improve maternal welfare, maternity and other benefits, tackle infant mortality, and push for housing provision.

- **Peace and internationalism**; Mary Agnes (Molly) Hamilton was an ardent peace campaigner before and during her time as an MP. Most of the Labour women MPs in the 1920s and 1930s were pacifist and internationalist following their experiences of WWI, many showing active support for the republicans in the Spanish Civil War.

- **Education**: Leah Manning was President of the National Union of Teachers before entering the House of Commons. Since education was one of the few careers open to women at this time, many of the first Labour women MPs had worked in this field. It became an increasingly important political issue during the 1920s and 1930s, culminating with the 1944 Education Act.

Before reaching the conclusion, chapter six will focus on how women established a position and a place within the House of Commons and the Labour Party. It will feature a bright green dress, a demand for bathing facilities and cross-party friendships. For those unable to wait, please feel free to skip straight to chapter six, but do return to the first five chapters as there is intrigue aplenty to keep you engaged, including the thrilling tale of one of the first women Labour MPs going undercover!

The Conclusion will then bridge the gap between then and now, by offering comparisons of life as a female MP at the beginning of the 1900s and that of MPs now. It is interesting to recognise that while there has been a great deal of progress, some of the challenges faced by our pioneers still exist today despite the complex changes in the world over the last one hundred years.

The UK of the early 1900s was a very different place for women than the UK of today. The majority of you will already know that women achieved the franchise in 1918. However, it only applied to women over the age of thirty who met the 'property requirement', or were married to a man that did. Full, equal voting rights with men were not granted until 1929, with the general election that year named the 'flapper election' in recognition of the large numbers of women who could - and did - vote. Additionally, it was not until the Sex Discrimination Act of 1920 that women had access to the legal and accounting professions. Perhaps most astonishingly of all, women were not considered 'persons' in their own right until 1929, by order of the Privy Council, a position that would - quite rightly - be a complete anathema to the majority of women living in the UK today.

In an interesting twist, from 1918 to 1929 women were able to stand for Parliament but were unable to vote. Jennie Lee was only twenty-three when she stood as the North Lanark Labour candidate in an early 1929 by-election, just prior to the change in voting rules and that year's general election.

As the majority of women who did not qualify for the vote prior to 1929 came from the working classes, female Labour MPs elected before this date had to balance the specific interests of working-class women, with what were perceived as wider Labour and working-class interests - and predominantly male interests. All men could, of course, already vote. This placed certain restrictions on how outspoken these early women MPs could be on particular issues.

The 1920s was a period of extraordinary political volatility. The 1923 general election produced a hung parliament, affording the young Labour Party, still only twenty-three years old, its first taste of power. The result – Labour 191 seats, the Liberal Party 158 seats and 258 for Conservatives - led to the formation of an informal Labour-Liberal coalition. Ramsay MacDonald, the Labour Leader, became the Party's first Prime Minister in January 1924. Yet given that the Labour and Liberal Parties were competing for the same sections of the electorate, the coalition quite simply could not last. Less than a year later another election followed. This time the Conservatives won a healthy majority with 412 seats to Labour's 151. The Labour loss of 40 seats was, however, nothing compared to the Liberal wipe-out. Reduced to only 40 MPs, the Liberals never truly recovered. The two-party system we have seen dominate politics over recent decades can, in fact, be linked to the events of 1924.

The very first woman to be elected to the House of Commons won her seat in the 1918 General Election. Countess Constance de Markievicz represented Sinn Fein for the Dublin St Patrick's constituency - whilst imprisoned in Holloway Prison. She, like others of Sinn Fein, did not take up her seat. Countess de Markievicz was one of only seventeen women to stand in 1918, out of a total of 1,623 candidates. As the Countess did not grace the House of Commons with her presence, Viscountess Nancy Astor is often cited as the first female MP. Astor, a Conservative MP, won a by-election for Plymouth Sutton in 1919 after her husband had to forfeit the seat on elevation to his father's peerage. The first Liberal woman MP was Margaret Wintringham, who was returned for Louth in 1921. Astonishingly Margaret won her seat without having spoken in public throughout the entire campaign. This

OUR WOMEN M.P's. 1923 ELECTION

YOU SENT THEM LAST TIME

SEND OTHERS WITH THEM NOW

Margaret Bondfield Northampton

Susan Lawrence North East Ham

Dorothy Jewson Norwich

1924 General Election Poster

was out of respect for her recently deceased husband, who was the former MP for Louth. One wonders if such tactics might work today!

The Labour Party was successful in returning women MPs to the House of Commons in 1923. This was the first General Election in which Labour successfully won the popular vote in significant enough numbers forming a minority government. The first three Labour women elected to the House of Commons - Margaret Bondfield (Northampton), Susan Lawrence (East Ham North) and Dorothy Jewson (Norwich) – entered parliament following the general election in December 1923. From very different social backgrounds, each would fly the flag for Labour in Parliament with the commitment one would expect of pioneers.

Sadly these three women lost their seats when the Labour-Liberal coalition collapsed less than a year later, although they did remain the flag-bearers for future women MPs. Dorothy Jewson never returned to politics, but Margaret Bondfield and Susan Lawrence were re-elected for Wallsend and East Ham North in by-elections in 1926. A fourth woman, Ellen Wilkinson, did in fact win Middlesborough East in 1924. These four women, as well as those others returned to the House of Commons during the inter-war years, were extraordinary people, true trailblazers who sought to position women not just within the Labour Party but on the national political stage.

Ellen Wilkinson, Labour MP for Middlesborough East, in 1925 with trade union colleagues

Even though they came from different social and economic backgrounds, each of the first four Labour women to sit in the Commons had been active in women's politics prior to standing for Parliament. It was therefore inconceivable that, once elected, they would feel no loyalty towards their sex and put their previous priorities behind them. However, as MPs they had to remain aware of the demands of their constituents and keep on the right side of the party whips. Softly, softly was the sensible approach.

Looking at the history of these four incredible women, it is not difficult to recognise the courage and determination that took them to the top. Margaret Bondfield, who became an MP in 1923, had been a leading light in the fight to improve the lives and status of working-class women for more than twenty-five years. She was one of the most effective and tenacious advocates of her generation and was the first woman to achieve cabinet status. Undoubtedly she was the most successful, if not the most high profile, of the first Labour women MPs, a true champion.

The number of Labour women in the House of Commons from 1918 to 1945 reached a maximum of only fifteen at any one time, but the first four Labour women MPs had over eighty years of political experience between them by the time they entered the House of Commons. What is more, much of that experience had been

Dorothy Jewson when an organiser for the National
Federation of Women Workers

gained campaigning on behalf of women. Almost all of Margaret Bondfield's work between 1898 and 1923 had been with women's organisations in one form or another. Dorothy Jewson was an organiser for the National Federation of Women Workers and then worked in the women's section of the General and Municipal Workers' Union. Susan Lawrence was an active campaigner for women in the workplace. Ellen Wilkinson had also been active in the women's suffrage movement.

'I feel sometimes that I am the Member for widows rather than the Member for Middlesbrough', Ellen Wilkinson told MPs on 22nd February 1928, when representing the cause of women over seventy who had been excluded from the government's pension scheme. Like most Labour MPs at this time, Ellen championed both women's interests and the interests of her class. In the mid-1920s when the split between the old, more radical feminism and the inter-war softly softly approach became evident, Ellen Wilkinson and her Labour women parliamentary colleagues were clear that their aim was to defend the party while seeking to limit economic exploitation for both men and women. When in March 1944 Ellen Wilkinson had to choose between backing equal pay or supporting the wartime coalition government, she backed the government in three confidence votes on the matter.

Nevertheless, the emphasis placed on women's campaigns by the first Labour women MPs came about in part because of the way the Labour Party and trade unions were organised during the 1920s and 1930s, which in turn reflected the social norms of the time. During the inter-war years working class men and women lived quite separate lives, just as they had ever since the industrial revolution. Men had paid work, while the woman's role was a domestic one, looking after the children and running the home. This division of labour was as clear cut for industrial workers as it was for the 'upstairs-downstairs' classes, with the possible exception of the textile industry where women worked in the mills.

The term working-class had real meaning then. While the rigid divisions of the Victorian era began slowly eroding following the First World War, Britain was still very much divided along class lines. Cities had working-class districts, usually where factories, docks and shipyards were located. The growing middle-class occupied an ever-expanding suburbia, while those who were very wealthy had their own enclaves.

The classification 'working-class' therefore had much more potency than 'working people', the phrase more often used after the Second World War. Working-class in the 1920s and 1930s referred to those who did manual, industrial jobs and their dependants. Some service sector employment may have been implied in the term, but working-class essentially meant industrial. The trade unions at the time saw themselves as representing the working class, and individual trade union members described themselves as such. The Labour Party gained the vast majority of its support from the working-class and was largely made up of male industrial workers and their families. The Party's very name came from its origins as the parliamentary wing of the trade union movement - established as the Labour Representation Committee in 1900 –and which sought to gain seats in Parliament for organised labour. Labour truly representing labour.

It was, inevitably, labour of the mainly male variety. Women failed to gain any real position in Labour politics before 1918 because membership of the Labour Party was possible only through an affiliated trade union or socialist society. The unintended consequence of the way the Labour Party was originally set up was that few women were eligible to join. Although women came in after the First World War, the Labour Party remained dominated by the main industrial trade unions which were, inevitably, male bastions.

Men and women were separated within the Labour Party structure just as they were in their daily lives. The 1918 reorganisation set up women's sections at constituency level; regional women's committees with a woman paid as Party organiser in each region; a national women's advisory committee; and four (later five) women on the Party's powerful National Executive Committee. There was also an annual conference of Labour women. This separate structure meant, in practice, that women were not seen as part of the mainstream, they represented an 'optional extra' with little or no say on any serious issues. Thus the notion of 'separate spheres' for women and men remained entrenched.

The years 1929 – 1931 were some of the worst in peacetime during the whole of the twentieth century. By the summer of 1931 the economic crisis following the Wall Street Crash had split the Labour Cabinet. Labour Prime Minister Ramsey Macdonald wanted to cut unemployment benefit, but was opposed by a large section of the Cabinet. The Government resigned on 23rd August 1931. The following day Macdonald announced he would lead an all-party National Government. The subsequent General Election held in October 1931 was a disaster for Labour. The Conservatives won a landslide with four hundred and seventy-three seats to Labour's fifty-two, and thirty-three for the Liberals. National Labour and National Liberal held forty-eight seats between them. Every single Labour woman MP lost her seat in this election. This collapse shows very clearly that the Labour Party did not select women in the safest seats. The 1931 general election was, in fact, reminiscent of the one held in 1924, in that the Labour women lost their seats when the electoral advantage turned against the Labour Party.

Labour women returned to the House of Commons in dribs and drabs during the 1930s, though most of those who were MPs during the 1920s never returned. Both Margaret Bondfield and Susan Lawrence, the female stars of the 1924 Labour Government, were destined never to be MPs again. Margaret Bondfield's story once she left parliament was one of personal tragedy. Standing again in Wallsend she was defeated in the 1935 general election. She was subsequently selected to stand in Reading for an election expected in 1939 or 1940, which, of course, never happened.

Margaret Bondfield's career in the House of Commons thus came to an end in 1931. The loss of what she describes as her life's work doomed Margaret to a breakdown. Though often circumspect in her autobiography, rarely delving deeply into her state of mind, she acknowledges that her post-election condition was less attributable to the strains of campaigning than 'the wretched split in the Party'. Margaret's malaise manifested itself physically, and she was confined to bed with acute muscle pain. This sad end to what had been a truly glittering parliamentary career only serves to remind us just how difficult life was for the few brave women who pioneered Labour women's representation in the House of Commons.

Margaret Bondfield died at Verecroft Nursing Home, Sanderstead, on 16th June 1953, having, despite her ill health, continued to serve as the Chief Women's Officer of General and Municipal Workers until 1938. When she did eventually retire she claims to have taken it well, stating in her autobiography *A Life's Work*:

> "It is only when people are stuck in a dull and tedious job that they begin to tire of life. I have often been angry with life, but never bored with it. Now I am very pleased with life".

Meanwhile, most of those who had enjoyed fleeting parliamentary careers in the late 1920s, only to be defeated in 1931, did not manage to make it back to the House of Commons. While Ethel Bentham, Ruth Dalton, Mary Agnes Hamilton, Jennie Lee and Lady Lucy Noel-Buxton were re-elected in the 1945 Labour landslide, Cynthia Mosley and Edith Picton-Turbervill never became MPs again. And neither did the arch-establishment woman, Marion Phillips, who died of cancer in 1932. The last general election before the Second World War, held in 1935, saw Leah Manning elected as MP for Sunderland; she had won a seat in East Islington in

February 1931 but managed to hold it for just 8 months, losing it in October of the same year. Ellen Wilkinson also returned in the 1935 General Election as MP for Jarrow. Three other Labour women won by-elections – Agnes Hardie in 1937, plus Edith Summerskill and Jennie Adamson in 1938. Hence during the whole of the 1930s there were only five Labour women MPs, hardly any advance on the four elected in the early 1920s.

The 1930s were not a good time for Labour politics. The only election after 1931 prior to the Second World War took place in 1935. The National Government, now led by Stanley Baldwin, gained a substantial, albeit reduced, majority. As in 1931 the majority of MPs were Conservative, though Labour did make gains on their very poor 1931 result. The continuing electoral success of the National Government inevitably meant the times were not propitious for radical, feminist or even left-leaning politics.

In Opposition, the new female Labour MPs elected during the 1930s – Leah Manning (who succeeded Ethel Bentham in her seat), Agnes Hardie, Jennie Adamson and Edith Summerskill - kept a relatively low profile. The veteran Ellen Wilkinson published several well-received books, including two novels, *Clash*, a romance set against the General Strike and *The Division Bell Mystery*, which was based in Westminster. She also wrote *The Town that was Murdered* , her account of Jarrow in the mid-1930s, which came out in 1936. Beatrice Webb, a social reformer and co-founder of the London School of Economics and Political Science, predicted 'a big political career' for Wilkinson. Webb saw that she was becoming moulded for the Front Bench and eventually for office. Webb further thought that Wilkinson would make a good departmental minister, more efficient and popular than those earlier Labour stateswomen Susan Lawrence and Margaret Bondfield.

The first Labour women MPs exploited the advantages of the women's franchise to the utmost. Obviously successful, they achieved what in the 1920s and 1930s was considered the pinnacle of political achievement, a seat in the House of Commons. Inevitably these leading women had to make huge sacrifices both politically and in their private lives. Yet some managed a personal life on top of their parliamentary and constituency duties. Edith Summerskill married and had a daughter, Shirley, who also became a doctor and MP. Jennie Lee married Aneurin Bevan; Ruth Dalton (the shortest serving British female MP) was married to Hugh, later to become Chancellor of the Exchequer, and had a daughter. Cynthia Mosley was the first wife of Oswald and had three children. Agnes Hamilton also married and had children, while Dorothy Jewson married twice and Leah Manning was married before entering Parliament. Agnes Hardie married the brother of Kier Hardie, Labour's first MP, and Jennie Adamson married a fellow MP. Lastly Lady Noel-Buxton was also married and raised an impressive six children.

Yet despite their obvious fortitude and commitment, with the exception of the two years following the 1929 general election, Labour women MPs could be counted on the fingers of one hand. Women were a novelty and not always welcomed by their male counterparts. It was not an enviable position. Yet the Labour women MPs rose to the challenge, gaining ministerial positions in the two Labour governments during the inter-war years in 1924 and 1929. They were true pioneers, brave and special women who paved the way for Labour women in the twentieth century.

A quick look at their political profiles highlight a few additional compelling facts and figures. For instance, three of these amazing women collectively accumulated sixty-eight years as MPs. Jennie Lee clocked up twenty-seven years and five months, Edith Summerskill twenty-two years and nine months, and Ellen Wilkinson seventeen years and ten months. At the other end of the spectrum the three with the lowest accumulated time as MPs comes to just over two years, with Ruth Dalton in office for just three months, Dorothy Jewson at ten months and Ethel Bentham with one year and seven months. The youngest to become an MP was Jennie Lee, who was just twenty-four years of age. The oldest was Ethel Bentham who was an impressive sixty-eight when she became an MP. The average age was a very respectable forty-five years.

With rich and varied backgrounds these women were fascinating both as politicians and as individuals. Their experiences, both on and off the political stage, make for an engaging and often exciting narrative.

CHAPTER 1
The Campaign for Birth Control

"I have women's issues to look after, but I do not want to be regarded purely as a women's MP... men voters dominate Middlesbrough East, thousands are unemployed, and I mean to stand up to the gruelling work for all their sakes"

Ellen Wilkinson, Yorkshire Evening News, 10 December 1924

The Labour Party constitution agreed in 1918 inevitably reflected the dominance of men in British, and indeed western society, at the time. Those new Labour women MPs who were seeking to establish their credentials and build a reputation therefore faced an almost insurmountable challenge. Virtually all of these strong and brave women believed that the best way to establish themselves was to show support for a broad range of topics and not just those perceived to be 'women's issues'. This was especially important within the Labour Party, whose male-dominated establishment found it hard to take on board the changing role of women. Of course the irony was that for many of these MPs, it was the poor representation of specialist women's issues that had been their catalyst for wanting to play an active role in politics. One of these issues – the demand for readily available, cost effective access to birth control, was to loom large for working-class and Labour women during the 1920s and 1930s.

All four of the first Labour women MPs were single when elected. Margaret Bondfield, Susan Lawrence and Ellen Wilkinson remained so, while Dorothy Jewson married twice after ceasing to be an MP. Whatever their personal preferences, marriage for these women at the beginning of the 1920s was at the very least a difficult prospect, becoming increasingly impossible as unemployment rose during the 1920s and 1930s, creating demands that women cease paid work after marriage – and freed up potential jobs for men. Mariage for these women would mean the end of their roles as MPs.

The women MPs also had to put up with appalling public commentary. On 20th

May 1926 the *Daily News* came up with this not so subtle sexual innuendo:

> "Ellen Wilkinson, till quite recently the only spinster in the House of Commons, has red hair and very Red opinions....The question arises whether celibacy has the same effect on women in politics as that which it exercises on public men." [1]

Interestingly this statement says as much about the perceived shortcomings of men as it does women.

Almost without exception, the women who pioneered women's political emancipation in the Labour movement had to make sacrifices, and the first four Labour women MPs were no exception. These sacrifices applied to both their political activity as MPs and their private lives. Just as marriage was out of the question, so were political stands which were perceived to be too radical or too woman-centred. Margaret Bondfield, for example, may have been romantically linked to Women's Trade Union League Secretary Mary Macarthur. Such was the imperative need for discretion during this period that we will probably never definitively know one way or the other.

Once in Parliament the first four, with the possible exception of Dorothy Jewson, became MPs and socialists first, and campaigners on behalf of women second. This was only to be expected. Political constraints notwithstanding, being one of the first four was achievement in itself and parliamentary and constituency business was obviously their priority. They also had to take account of the Labour Party attitude to women's issues, which was not always sympathetic or helpful. Bondfield, Lawrence and Wilkinson also appeared to see the potential for a career in Labour politics. In 1924 Margaret Bondfield rose to be Britain's first woman cabinet minister, while Susan Lawrence was appointed a junior minister at the Department of Health. Ellen Wilkinson later became Secretary of State for Education in the 1945 Labour Government.

To understand these women and their political positions, including their stance on birth control, it is important to know what influences helped form their tenacity and determination. The eleventh child of textile factory workers, a young Margaret Bondfield left home at fourteen to serve an apprenticeship in a large draper's shop in Hove, East Sussex, run by one of her sister's friends. She did not see her family home again until she was nineteen; the effect of this five year separation at such a young age can only be imagined. In 1894 Margaret went to live in London with her brother Frank, working in another shop. It was during this period that she began to take an active interest in politics.

Margaret was appointed assistant general secretary of the Shop Assistants' Union in 1898, having been rapidly elected to the District Council of the Union, and was also on the executive of the Women's Trade Union League. She produced a report for the Women's Industrial Council into the pay and conditions of shop workers in the same year, becoming the leading expert on this issue. Her work,

Margaret Bondfield age 14 when she
began her apprenticeship

however, was not universally accepted and Margaret put her own career on the line during the course of this report - even being forced to go undercover for a time. Margaret Bondfield's energy and commitment certainly manifested themselves at a young age.

In 1906, Bondfield and Mary Macarthur, one of the country's most energetic campaigners for working-class women, established the first general union for women, the National Federation of Women Workers (NFWW). Margaret's involvement did not stop there. As Chairwoman of the Adult Suffrage Society she vehemently opposed the notion that females should initially be granted only a limited franchise, arguing that this would be detrimental to working class women. Bondfield's interests were by this time clearly leaning towards elective politics, and in 1908 she resigned from the Shop Assistants' Union to become secretary of the Women's Labour League, the forerunner of the Labour Party women's sections. She was also active in the Women's Co-operative Guild.

Bondfield maintained her involvement in women's campaigns throughout the First World War, joining forces with the Women's Freedom League to establish the Women's Peace crusade, which called for a negotiated peace. Returning to the question of votes for women in 1916, Margaret set up a new National Council for Adult Suffrage with Women's Trade Union League Secretary Mary Macarthur and George Lansbury, a leading campaigner for women's suffrage and future Labour Leader. The Council's main aim was to persuade the government to reconsider its plans for a limited extension of the franchise.

Though not as deeply involved in women's issues as Margaret Bondfield, Susan Lawrence also met Mary Macarthur and spent the years between 1912 - when she joined the Women's Trade Union League - and her election as an MP in 1923, campaigning for the working-class female cause. As well as helping organise women workers, Lawrence co-wrote two books on the subject, *Women in the Engineering Trades* (1917) and *Labour Women and International Legislation* (1919).

Unlike Bondfield, Lawrence was born to wealthy parents. The young Susan Lawrence was educated at University College, London and Newnham College, Cambridge. She was originally a strong Conservative. However all this changed when Susan Lawrence became aware of the appalling deprivation in the working-class areas of London, particularly the low wages earned by the charwomen and

Margaret Bondfield (right) at the Women's Labour League Conference in 1910 with Mary Middleton (left) and Mary Macarthur (centre)

cleaners who maintained London's schools. According to the Manchester Guardian (25th October 1947):

> "What she learned shocked her and she moved from right to left overnight, changing not only her politics but her dress and her way of life." [2]

Encouraged by Beatrice and Sydney Webb, Susan joined the Fabian Society in 1911 and the Labour Party a year later. Even though she never lost her upper-class demeanour, Susan Lawrence earned the confidence of Labour Party members, being elected to the London County Council in 1913 and Poplar Council in 1919, where she served until 1924. Her sincerity was such that her Tory past proved no barrier. Moreover, one of her main concerns during her Conservative years was education, a topic dear to Labour hearts.

In common with Margaret Bondfield, Lawrence was already an experienced politician by the time she entered Parliament. She had, in fact, almost done it all in the twenty-eight years before she arrived at Westminster – gained an education, been a London County Councillor, changed parties, gone to prison for her beliefs, as well as working with and for working-class and Labour women.

The other Labour woman elected in 1923, Dorothy Jewson, also had a privileged background. Educated at Cheltenham Ladies' College, Dorothy returned to Norwich after completing her degree at Girton College, Cambridge and acquiring a teaching qualification, working in a boarding school in the city. Together with her brother, she carried out a large-scale investigation into poverty, published under the title *The Destitute of Norwich*.

Jewson also had connections with Mary Macarthur, who invited Dorothy to become an organiser for the National Federation of Women's Workers (NFWW) in 1916. While there, Jewson worked closely with Margaret Bondfield, demonstrating the close links between the first Labour women MPs and leading women in the wider labour movement. When the NFWW amalgamated with the National Union of General and Municipal Workers in 1921, Jewson was employed in the newly formed women's section. Like Bondfield, she was an opponent of Britain's involvement in the First World War, though she was perhaps more radical in referring to herself as a pacifist. Having been active in her local Labour Party in Norwich, Dorothy Jewson became the city's MP in 1923.

Ellen Wilkinson, known as 'Red Ellen' due to the colour of her hair as well as her politics, was elected at the time as Bondfield, Lawrence and Jewson lost their seats. Wilkinson also had a strong record in Labour and radical women's politics prior to arriving in Westminster. Returned in the general election of October 1924, slightly less than a year after the preceding election when Bondfield, Lawrence and Jewson became MPs, Wilkinson was from a working-class background in Manchester. Since Wilkinson's father was a worker in a textile factory her social position was not unlike that of Bondfield.

Born in 1891, Wilkinson won a scholarship to Manchester University where she was active in the University Socialist Federation. She joined the National Union of Women's Suffrage Societies (NUWSS) in 1912, becoming a district organiser a year later. She was also a member of the Fabian Society. Three years later in July 1915, Ellen was employed by the National Union of Distributive and Allied Workers as its first woman organiser. Ellen joined the Communist Party on its formation in Britain in 1920 and managed to fight Ashton-under-Lyme in the 1923 election as the official Labour candidate (while still a Communist). She was also active in local politics, and was elected to serve on Manchester City Council in 1923. A year after resigning her Communist Party membership, Ellen became MP for Middlesbrough East, proving a colourful, irreverent but passionate member of the House of Commons.

Bondfield, Lawrence, Jewson and Wilkinson were true pioneers. The first four Labour women MPs had over eighty years of political experience between them by the time they entered the House of Commons. What is more, much of that experience had been gained campaigning on behalf of women. Almost all of Margaret Bondfield's work between 1898 and 1923 had been with women's organisations. Susan Lawrence, while not especially remembered for her work for women, was nonetheless an active campaigner for women in the workplace. Dorothy Jewson was an organiser for the National Federation of Women Workers, and then worked in the women's section of the General and Municipal Workers'

Union. Ellen Wilkinson had been active in the women's suffrage movement.

There is one campaign, perhaps more than any other, which illustrated the constraints, both personal and political, on the first Labour women MPs. The fight for birth control for working-class women places the forces arrayed against Bondfield, Lawrence, Jewson and Wilkinson in sharp relief. Men and women were separated within the Labour Party structure just as they were in their daily lives. The Party's separate structure for women meant that they had virtually no say, let alone influence, on Party policy. Nowhere was this state of affairs more apparent than the issue of birth control for working-class women, which was repeatedly supported by Labour women at their annual conference, but opposed by the party establishment at the national Labour Party conference. This created a very real dilemma for the Labour women MPs. Though Bondfield, Lawrence and Wilkinson were supportive, only Dorothy Jewson was prepared to stick her neck out and stand opposed to the established order. And though a lone female Labour voice in Parliament, Jewson was not alone in the wider Labour Party and other working-class female organisations.

The demand for birth control for working-class women, as opposed to wealthier women who already had access to such provision, came to the fore after the First World War. Once Marie Stopes opened up the birth control question, much of its social stigma disappeared, at least for the middle classes. Middle-class women gained access to contraception because they could pay. Working-class women with large families on the other hand, could often barely afford food and rent let alone contraception. The prevailing attitudes to class had just as much effect on limiting family size as every other aspect of life in the inter-war years. In the days before the National Health Service only those who could afford it received comprehensive medical treatment, and birth control came into that category. Better-off married women were able to pay for contraception - poorer women were not.

Moreover, Marie Stopes, author of the two books which brought birth control into the open, *Married Love* and *Wise Parenthood*, targeted her message at middle-class women. The book *Married Love* "was quite frankly based on observation of, and addressed to, the educated, prosperous and privileged classes," said Stella Browne, one of the leading campaigners for universal access to birth control. [3] To her credit, Marie Stopes went on to produce *Planned Parenthood*, which was aimed more squarely at working class women.

Yet despite her middle-class outlook, Marie Stopes received hundreds of letters from across the class divide. Poorer women often talked in class terms:

"I feel it is a great injustice and unchristian-like to think that rich women should have this knowledge and a poor woman should live in ignorance of it." [And] "The poor people of this land cry out in anguish for this knowledge which the aristocracy and capitalists would have withheld. …the upper classes have had birth control long enough, they would like to make it appear it is only the working-class man and wife who come together." [4]

The anguish contained in these letters speaks to us down the years. Working-class women were suffering because they were denied what was available to the wealthy. There was, however, another less palatable side to this issue. Seemingly uncontrolled fertility was regarded as an inevitable aspect of working class experience, a reflection and result of an almost intrinsic inability to exercise the restraint thought to underpin middle class morality. In other words, it was acceptable for middle class women to have sex because they were capable of being responsible about it. Working-class women seemed incapable of acting in this same, upright fashion [5]. Those who championed birth control for the working classes faced the prospect of social ostracism at the very least. Mr D.W. from Lancashire, who wrote to Marie Stopes in 1925, explained it like this:

> "Since I commenced a ruthless war on poverty and distress by advocating the principle of scientific birth control, my employers have hurled me into the surplus labour army…" [6]

While it may have suited sections of the bourgeoisie and ruling establishment to castigate working-class females, it is nonetheless true that these women were woefully ignorant, through no fault of their own, about almost everything to do with sex. Sex itself was a taboo subject for all but the very bold, making discussion of birth control virtually impossible. Some-time Labour Party member and birth control champion Dora Russell wrote after one visit to a women's group in Motherwell in 1925:

> "The women blush and are terrified when they hear me say things that they dare not say themselves. The strength of a taboo is a thing one scarcely recognises until one gets among people like these – wives who would really sooner die than complain of intimate pains to their husbands." [7]

Furthermore Stella Browne considered that women's sexual ignorance was the product of, amongst other things:

> "the tyrannous demand for theoretical ignorance and even anatomical virginity of the bride".

Sexual knowledge of any kind was often seen as unrespectable, and therefore generally regarded as the province of men [8], who were more likely to encounter it, or to learn how to obtain it.

The inevitable result of sexual ignorance was large numbers of children. Since public health reforms had improved infant mortality, women had to care for ever larger families. In the debate in the House of Commons on the birth control bill in 1926, the bill's sponsor, East End MP Earnest Thurtle, told MPs:

> "We are expending money in broadcasting information about sanitation, personal hygiene, diet and matters of that sort. We are expending money about tuberculosis and venereal disease, and we are doing that solely on the ground

of maintaining public health. The Ministry of Health itself is engaged in a fight on behalf of national fitness, and there is not a phase of that fight which is not made more difficult by the fact that in the very poorest districts women are having much larger families than is good either for them or for the state." [9]

Judging by what little was ever said, working-class women perceived male sexuality to be largely predatory. In its testimony to the Minister of Health in 1924, the Workers' Birth Control Group used "Mrs F" as a typical example of a working-class mother: "aged 34 [18 pregnancies]… refuses coitus with her husband until he overpowers her." [10] Working-class women of this time were apt to view a good husband as one who left his wife alone sexually. A bad husband was unable to control his desires. What is more, letters sent to Marie Stopes make it clear that husbands were often unwilling to co-operate with birth control practices.

Ishbel Macdonald, daughter of Ramsey Macdonald, Labour's first Prime Minister, explained future MP Ethel Bentham's reluctance to give advice on birth control thus:

"…she [Ethel] told me privately that one reason she was against it [birth control] was if he knew the risk of his actions were less likely to lead to pregnancy, a husband felt at liberty to overtax or molest his wife unreasonably." [11]

That Ethel Bentham did not wish her thoughts about men and sex to be aired openly speaks volumes about attitudes to sex at the time. It was not to be discussed, and was a subject men and women found difficult to talk about with each other. Mainly because of this, the birth control campaign for working-class women was fought almost entirely on the issue of maternal and child health, a matter of some concern as the rate of maternal mortality actually increased between 1921 and 1926 from 3.91 per 1000 births to 4.2/1000. [12] The leading campaigners rightly saw the well-being of mothers and children as the only way to make any progress. Reformers such as Dora Russell (wife of Bertrand), who wished to improve women's experience of sex and sexual activity, spoke almost exclusively to the middle-classes. The urgent matter for working-class women was to limit the number of children they would bear.

By 1922 the Co-operative Women's Guild, probably the leading working-class organisation campaigning on behalf of women, was actively discussing birth control, as were some Labour women's organisations. Birth control champion Stella Browne, who made a point of touring working class women's groups, reported being approached by elderly women saying:

"You've come too late to help me, Comrade, but give me some papers for my girls. I don't want them to have the life I've had." [13]

The majority of grassroots women in the Labour Party were pro-birth control, though there were some in influential positions, notably the Chief Woman Officer

Marion Phillips, who were very opposed. Although this opposition was more for pragmatic, political than moral reasons, the fact that Phillips took the side of the Labour Party male establishment was not at all helpful in furthering the demand for birth control.

At the same time as the British birth control movement was underway, the United States was also looking to educate women on contraception, a key catalyst being the number of men who returned from the First World War with venereal diseases. Contraception, targeted as a public health issue by the government, began to lose some of its stigma which allowed campaigners of women's issues, such as Margaret Sanger, to refocus the government's message towards women's health. As well as recognising the health issues, Sanger wanted women to be able to take greater control of when they had children, to allow them to gain the freedom necessary to play a greater role in society and on their own terms.

Closer to home, contraception was not legalised in France until 1967, despite the country being one of the first to recognise the need to control birth rates, and around one hundred years earlier than in most other countries. In fact, contrary to the direction being taken by many countries, France passed a law in 1920 banning any birth control education.

Following the 1923 Labour women's conference, Dorothy Jewson, Dora Russell, Frida Laski, plus another two hundred women from the Labour Party and the Independent Labour Party, came together in an informal committee to disseminate birth control information in the Labour movement. Fresh from an unsuccessful deputation to Labour Health Minister John Wheatley, Labour birth control campaigners at the Women's Conference had to endure Marion Phillips's opposition to birth control, and a vague statement from the Labour Party National Executive Committee (NEC) suggesting that socialism would provide all the answers. Both Phillips and the NEC cited the Catholic vote, which they believed would turn away from the Labour Party if it supported birth control. Labour women, however, had little truck with this argument, as they were certain many Catholic women were on their side [14].

The Workers' Birth Control Group (WBCG) was officially established in 1924 to campaign for birth control, espousing Labour Party values as distinct from those of the Malthusians and Eugenicists who had long advocated family limitation only among the "inferior" classes. Dorothy Jewson, still an MP, became its president, and Dora Russell took up the important post of secretary. The other two Labour women MPs at this time, Margaret Bondfield and Susan Lawrence, joined the Group, as did Ellen Wilkinson. However, Bondfield, Lawrence and Wilkinson were only paper members; there is no record of them providing active support for the birth control movement. In a way this is not too surprising. The parliamentary careers of Bondfield and Lawrence began to take off both achieving junior ministerial posts in the Labour minority government which took office in January 1924. Susan Lawrence wrote articles on maternal health and education in *The Labour Woman*.

Birth control had always been a difficult issue in the male-dominated Labour

A rare cartoon of Susan Lawrence

Party. The men, on the whole, did not think it important, while the Party establishment was afraid of the reaction of the Roman Catholic Church and the Party's Catholic supporters, foreseeing electoral damage in those parliamentary seats with large Catholic populations. There was, in addition, real ambivalence from women members of the Labour Party. A letter from a woman called Lillie Turner to *The Labour Woman* in 1924, puts forward an alternative view:

"My difficulty is that birth control does not get to the root of the trouble today. We, as Labour and Socialist women, are out first for a new social order, and we believe that through our practical socialist programme we can achieve a full and free life for every man, woman and child....I give credit to the purpose of the ladies who advocate birth control....But is this not a side issue, and may we not be very easily stampeded from the great questions that really matter?"

The WBCG was not to be put off. The Group's focus was on pressing for state provision, and it was avowedly political from its inception. Rooted in working-class concerns, it viewed the question of birth control in terms of class – a vital aspect of the Labour and socialist struggle. The WBCG saw birth control as an essential part of the entire welfare package and the key to giving women greater control over their lives. The WBCG therefore put enhancing motherhood at the centre of its programme and policies. Its stated objectives were:

- To strengthen public opinion among workers as to the importance of birth control in any scheme of social progress

- To bring within the reach of working people the best and most scientific information on birth control

- To bring pressure to bear through Parliament, and otherwise, on the Ministry of Health, to recognise birth control as an essential part of public health work, and therefore allow information to be given by the local health authorities to their child welfare centres [15]

The emphasis on maternal and child welfare was, of course, all about married women. Children born out of wedlock were probably even more taboo than the sex act itself in the 1920s and 1930s. As such, illegitimate children never appeared in the birth control discourse. Single women fared little better in terms of social acceptance or recognition, unless they possessed some degree of social status. This was, of course, the case with the first four female Labour MPs, whose standing was significantly higher than that enjoyed by Members of Parliament today. However, one could argue that since all of them were single while in Parliament, they may have lacked natural empathy for this issue and that could have contributed to the failure of all except Jewson to be actively involved in the WBCG and the struggle for birth control.

The Workers' Birth Control Group was however knocking on an increasingly open door. By 1924 there was a growing acceptance of the idea that contraception should be available to all married women, irrespective of their ability to pay. The turning point had in fact come three years earlier, in 1921. Marie Stopes opened the first birth control clinic, the Mothers' Clinic for Constructive Birth Control, in March of that year, and the Malthusian League, the birth control movement's forerunner established in 1877, set up a centre for contraceptive instruction. More importantly in terms of popular acceptance, the King's physician, Lord Dawson, gave outspoken support for birth control in a 1921 address to a lay congress of the Church of England. Despite his own strong Anglican faith, he claimed:

"...the love envisaged by the Lambeth Conference (is)... an invertebrate, joyless thing – not worth having". [16]

Marie Stopes's clinic was ground-breaking indeed. Situated in Holloway, the Mothers' Clinic for Constructive Birth Control provided free consultations, and contraceptives sold at cost price or provided free of charge if the women could not afford to pay. It was available to all married women, catering for five thousand patients by 1924. Stopes's aims, set out in her analysis of these first five thousand cases, were to test the belief that the working-classes were hostile to birth control, to obtain first-hand facts about contraception in practice, and to collect scientific data on the sex life of women [17].

Despite her highly laudable activities during the 1920s and 1930s in making contraception available to women of all classes, one of her motivations was a strong belief in eugenics as a Darwinian means of improving society. An extreme example of her views was the opposition to her son's marriage on the grounds his fiancée had poor eyesight. In an ironic twist, despite his well-documented desire for genetic purity and the place eugenics had in engineering this, Hitler had all of Stopes's books burned when he came to power in Germany.

Discussions regarding birth control as a means of guiding social development played a meaningful part in the broader debate. A number of leading figures in the UK at that time spoke positively on the benefits of social control. Leading economist John Maynard Keynes served as Director of the British Eugenics Society and stated that eugenics was:

> "…the most important, significant and, I would add, genuine branch of society which exists." [18]

This focus on improving the societal status of the UK was used by some as a means of promoting birth control for the working classes.

Regardless of Stopes's motivation, as more voluntary clinics were set up – by 1926 the Society for the Provision of Birth Control Clinics (formerly the Malthusian Walworth Women's Welfare Centre) had eight affiliated clinics - the opposition to birth control became organised. In 1922, Halliday Sutherland, a Catholic doctor, published *Birth Control: A Statement of Christian Doctrine against the Neo-Malthusians*, accusing Stopes of "experimenting on the poor". Stopes sued for libel. Though at first successful, this decision was overturned on appeal and then in the House of Lords.

Two further incidents fuelled the birth control campaign. In 1923 Nurse Daniels, a member of the Eugenics Society, was dismissed from her post in Edmonton for giving out contraceptive advice, while communist-anarchists Guy Aldred and Rose Witcop were prosecuted for selling Margaret Sanger's *Family Limitation*. The publication was deemed to be obscene and all copies destroyed. Aldred and Witcop did, however, have influential friends, their legal fees being paid by Dora Russell and the aforementioned economist JM Keynes.

The Labour victory in the 1923 general election caused a surge of optimism in the birth control movement. In the spring of that year, the Ministry of Health published *Maternal Mortality*, which reported that three thousand women died in childbirth each year, and that pregnancy held greater risk for exhausted mothers caring for large families. There was also increased Labour Party activity. Following the establishment of a minority Labour government in January 1924 two Labour controlled boroughs – Battersea and Stepney – were warned by the Ministry of Health that their grants would be withdrawn if their clinics, set up to provide maternity service, continued to give contraceptive advice.

The attitude of the Labour-run Ministry of Health sparked a deputation which presented a petition to the Health Minister, John Wheatley. The deputation, including Dora Russell, the author HG Wells, and former Labour MP Dorothy Jewson (who had recently lost her seat), presented a petition containing 6,056 signatures and urging freedom for maternity centres and public officials to give information on contraception. Though a Labour Minister, John Wheatley was also a Roman Catholic. He told the deputation that a clear distinction must be made between allowing access to knowledge and actually distributing it. He further said that public opinion would not permit state-aided institutions to do more than direct people to places where they might obtain information. The petition also included the names of twenty-two Labour MPs sympathetic to its aims. Interestingly, not one of the three female Labour MPs of the time – Bondfield, Lawrence and Wilkinson - was included [10].

More than anything else, it was Wheatley's response that galvanised Labour-supporting birth control campaigners to form the Workers' Birth Control Group. While all four of the first Labour women MPs became members of the WBCG, only the now ex-MP Dorothy Jewson was on the deputation to Wheatley. Bondfield, Lawrence and Wilkinson continued to demonstrate a striking ambivalence to one of the most important demands of working-class women and one of the key issues for the working-class women's organisations, despite the fact that all three had been heavily involved in the issue prior to their election.

This ambivalence almost certainly indicates just how fragile the position of Bondfield, Lawrence and Wilkinson actually was. While they felt able to support birth control in theory, in practice they realised that opposing Health Minister Wheatley, the Labour Party NEC and the Chief Woman Officer Marion Phillips, was not a sensible political stance.

The debate on birth control continued to rage in the Labour Party. In 1925 the National Executive Committee issued a statement declaring:

> "That the subject of birth control is in its nature one which should be made a political Party issue, but should remain a matter on which members of the Party should be free to hold and promote their individual convictions." [20]

Birth control was officially off the agenda at the 1926 Labour Party Conference under the rule that forbade discussion of any resolution which had already appeared at three Conferences in succession. Given this was the year of the General Strike, it is perhaps understandable that the Labour Party establishment did not want to muddy the waters with debates around birth control.

However, none of this was enough to put off the indomitable Dora Russell. At the 1926 Conference she made an impassioned plea, comparing birth control to the miners' demand for a seven hour day. The call to open the discussion was won by a narrow margin on a card vote: 1,656,000 for and 1,620,000 against. The miners supported the birth controllers, possibly because they wished to reward the loyalty of women during the General Strike. Mr Horner of the Miners' Federation told the Conference:

> "…the women had saved the British Labour Movement from disgrace. Had it not been for what the women had done, except for one or two unions, nothing would have been done." [21]

It was against this background that Labour Shoreditch MP Earnest Thurtle introduced his Ten Minute Rule Bill in 1926 – the Local Authorities (Birth Control) Enabling Bill.

> "…authorise local authorities to incur expenditure, when deemed expedient, in conveying knowledge of birth control methods to married women who desire it."

Thurtle, an indefatigable birth control campaigner who had raised the subject many times in Parliament, said he was motivated by a desire to "remove one of the disabilities of poverty." [22] Wealthy women had access to birth control information while the poor were denied this knowledge. Thurtle told MPs that the birth rate in prosperous Westminster and Chelsea was 11.2 and 14.3 per 1000 respectively, but in his own constituency of Shoreditch it was 25 per 1000. And yet poorer areas such as Shoreditch had less healthy populations and conditions were least suited to raising children.

However, Thurtle was no eugenicist, maintaining a strong humanitarian standpoint in his Commons speech:

> "It is said we are breeding from the wrong stock. I am not prepared to accept that. There is no reason to assume that the children of the working classes are one whit inferior, either physically or mentally, to the children of the better off classes. What is true is that as soon as they come into life they never get anything like equality of opportunity with the other classes."

Thurtle expanded his ideology later in the debate:

> "I am a Socialist, and I would be the last man to pretend that this restriction of families is any real cure for the root problem of poverty. The social inequalities and disabilities which afflict the mass of the poor people have their roots much deeper than this. But, even as a Socialist, I do say that knowledge which would enable working-class people to exercise a wide restriction in the size of their families would have an immediate ameliorative effect on the condition of those workers, and it is for that reason that, as a Socialist, I am prepared to advocate this Bill." [23]

Thurtle's Bill was merely permissive, enabling local authorities to act but not compelling them to do so. The Bill was predicated on the now generally accepted principle that it was desirable to spread information to reach and maintain national standards of health. The Ten Minute Rule procedure allows only one reply before moving to a division. The fact that the one opposing speech was delivered by a fellow Labour MP illustrates once again the deep divisions within Labour on the birth control issue.

Earnest Thurtle's opponent was the Reverend James Barr, a Presbyterian Minister who represented Motherwell where the first mother and baby clinic had been established. Barr's argument was in essence religious:

> "I believe that a bountiful Creator has provided ample resources for all, and that if we had only wise production and just distribution there would be ample for all the people." [24]

The following question was put and heavily defeated, Ayes 81 and Noes 167. Two thirds of the Noes came from the Labour benches:

"That leave be given to bring in a Bill to authorise local authorities to incur expenditure, when deemed expedient, in conveying knowledge of birth control methods to married women who desire it."

The birth controllers decided to try once more in the House of Lords and the cause was taken up by Lord Buckmaster, a pillar of the Establishment and very different from the radical Thurtle. On 26th April 1926, Buckmaster moved that local authority welfare centres be allowed to provide married women with information about family limitation. Buckmaster won the division in the Lords by fifty-seven votes to forty-four; both sides in the birth control divide had now won a parliamentary victory. Perhaps more importantly, by 1926 there were more than two thousand five hundred maternity and child welfare clinics, and the birth control policy of these institutions would undoubtedly have a major influence on birth control practice in the country. However, given the permissive nature of legislation, practices varied enormously. A few months after the parliamentary debates on birth control the Government admitted that thirty-seven local authorities and seventy-four other organisations had sent resolutions in favour of giving birth control advice in the mother and child welfare centres.

Women in the Labour Party meanwhile continued their campaign. Birth control was on the agenda of the 1928 National Conference of Labour Women, despite the NEC statement that "the subject of birth control is by its nature not one that should be made a political Party issue." Dora Russell argued that the NEC statement did not represent women's demands, that it was specious and evasive and that Labour women were deprived of the support of their own MPs. She also maintained that since the NEC should support the liberty of the individual, all maternity centres should be free to give advice and help to those who required it in support of that aim [25].

The reply by Arthur Henderson MP, a former Labour Leader, on behalf of the NEC was very revealing. Henderson claimed the NEC had given full consideration to birth control. It was a great social and economic question vital to the wellbeing of the mother, but it was also a great moral question. According to the Labour Party constitution, a two-thirds majority at the annual Conference was required to add any matter to the official programme - and if it were made a party matter, other parties would organise against it:

"If it is true that you cannot legislate in advance of public opinion, it is certainly true of this question which touches deep religious convictions of large numbers of people."

This view formed the core of Henderson's argument. [26]

Ellen Wilkinson MP, a nominal member of the Workers' Birth Control Group, took a very establishment line at this Labour Women's Conference in 1928. Breaking the vow of silence she appeared to have taken with Bondfield and Lawrence up to this point, Wilkinson told the Conference that birth control was not a class issue and therefore more likely to succeed if not narrowed to a Party matter. Wilkinson, according to her biographer Betty Vernon, was concerned that the large number of Roman Catholics in her constituency would turn away from Labour if she supported birth control, though this is not entirely convincing.

There was no doubt that the Labour Party was split on the issue, the NEC and most of the trade unions being against allowing free advice in local authority maternal welfare clinics, with the grassroots women passionately in favour. It was also true that when push came to shove Ellen Wilkinson spoke in favour of the NEC line, while the other prominent Labour women MPs remained silent.

Seven additional Labour women were elected to the House of Commons in 1929. Ruth Dalton and Jennie Lee were returned during that year in by-elections for Bishop Auckland and Lanark North respectively. Ethel Bentham (Islington North), Mary Hamilton (Blackburn), Lady Cynthia Mosley (Stoke-on Trent), Marion Phillips (Sunderland) and Edith Picton-Turbervill (The Wrekin) became MPs in the general election. This was the first election in which all women could vote following the extension of voting rights to achieve adult suffrage for everyone over the age of twenty-one. Lady Noel-Buxton won her North Norfolk seat in a by-election the following year.

The 1929 general election has gone down in history as the "flapper" election, in reference to the new cohort of young women voters. The Labour Party under Ramsey MacDonald won the most seats, but not an absolute majority, while Lloyd George's Liberals gained some of the ground they lost in 1924 and held the balance of power. Ramsey MacDonald decided to form a minority administration with himself as Prime Minister, a decision that was destined to prove fatal for Labour.

Sidney Webb, one of the leading lights of the Fabian Society, was created a peer, Lord Passfield, and elevated to the position of Colonial Secretary in the Government. He wrote about the difficulties faced by the second Labour Government:

> "The constant international complications involved alike in reparations and armaments, the world-wide industrial depression, the catastrophic collapse of prices, the ever present misery of chronic unemployment, the universal colossal taxation which has failed to avert a recurrence of deficits. The Labour Cabinet of 1929 – 31 stumbled through its share of these general troubles, aggravated in its own case by the special difficulties inherent in never having a majority in the House of Commons." [27]

However, the birth control campaign achieved a significant victory in the midst of all this chaos and suffering. Birth control organisations had pressured for state birth control advice in local authority clinics during the 1929 election. In 1930 the various organisations supporting birth control came together for a major public conference; *Birth Control by Public Health Authoritie*s. A resolution was sent to Public Health Minister Arthur Greenwood, hitherto ambivalent on the birth control issue. He finally gave way with Memorandum 153/MCW, which conceded that local authority clinics could give advice to mothers whose heath would be under threat with further pregnancies. The Memorandum stated:

> "It is not the function of the Centres to give advice in regard to birth control... [but] the Government considers that, in cases where there are *medical grounds* for giving advice on contraceptive methods to married women in attendance at the Centres, it may be given, but that such advice should be limited to *cases where further pregnancy would be detrimental to health*, and should be given at a separate session."

The Memorandum, issued without fanfare, was finally reprinted and officially circulated in 1931.

Now that the contraceptive battle was to all intents and purposes completed with the publication of Memorandum 153/MCW, one of the major working-class women's campaigns had reached a natural conclusion. However, the subject of limiting family size continued to exercise many in the Labour Party, since it remained an issue for working-class women despite the fall in the birth rate during the 1930s. The focus shifted towards abortion, an unspoken reality for many poor women. The subject had, in fact, been raised in the 1924 deputation to Health Minister John Wheatley:

> "Anyone with experience of work in the Labour movement or personal knowledge of working mothers can tell you that the working mother who does not admit in confidence to one or two deliberate "miscarriages" is the exception rather than the rule". [28]

The Labour Party establishment, never supportive of contraception, was completely hostile to abortion. Even the National Conference of Labour Women in 1935 only felt able to discuss abortion in the context of mental illness during pregnancy. *Labour Woman*, the organisation's official organ, completely ignored the 1937 Government Inter-Departmental Committee on abortion. Unsurprisingly there is no mention of any of the Labour women MPs actively supporting abortion during the 1930s.

The only working-class women's organisation to come out in favour of abortion reform was the Women's Co-operative Guild who passed a resolution at their 1934 conference "making of abortion a legal operation that can be carried under the same conditions of any other operation". By 1935 abortion law reform was widely discussed, with the middle-class National Council of Women passing a resolution urging the Government to establish an investigative committee. The Abortion Law Reform Association (ALRA) was formed at the beginning of 1936. Janet Chance, an advocate for sex education and an active abortion law reformer, became its first Chair, and the colourful, long-time birth control campaigner, Stella Browne,

Vice-Chair. Labour high-flier Frida Laski was also a founder member. Although the ALRA naturally looked towards the Labour Party, they made little headway. The energy and desire for change that was so apparent during the early 1920s had gone, dissipated in the morass of economic chaos, mass unemployment and the rise of fascism in continental Europe. Moreover, with the honourable exception of Edith Summerskill, who devoted a whole chapter of her autobiography, *A Woman's World* (1967), to birth control, the 1930s intake of Labour women MPs had virtually no interest in limiting family size.

That the first Labour women MPs felt restricted in offering their support to the birth control issue speaks volumes about the political culture of the time. As MPs they felt they had to follow the line taken by the Labour Party NEC, possibly because all of the first Labour women MPs had only a tenuous hold on their political careers. In this politically volatile period, all the women lost their seats at some point and only a few were re-elected. Moreover, since birth control was controversial with powerful bodies, particularly the Roman Catholic Church and other religious groupings, the women MPs felt they should tread carefully for fear of losing votes and their chances of re-election. Since all the Labour women MPs relied on their Commons' seats for their livelihoods, this was a powerful consideration and one which deserves to be recognised.

References:

1. Ellen Wilkinson *Scrapbook*, Book 3, May 1926 – December 1927

2. Martin Pugh, 'Class Traitors: Conservative Recruits to Labour, 1900 – 1930', 1998

3. International Journal of Ethics, quoted in Lesley Hall, The Life and Times of Stella Browne: Feminist and Free Spirit, 2011

4. Ruth Hall (ed) – Dear Dr Stopes: Sex in the 1920s, 1978

5. Stephen Brooke Bodies, *Sexuality and the "Modernisation" of the British Working Classes*, 1920s to 1960s, International Labor and Working Class History 2006

6. Dear Dr Stopes ibid

7. Quoted in Past and Present no 189

8. *Birth Control, Sex and Marriage in Britain*, 1918 – 1960, 2006

9. Hansard 1926

10. Quoted in Brooke ibid

11. Quoted in Christine Collette, For Labour and For Women, 1989

12. Dr Campbell's report on the Protection of Motherhood, quoted in Audrey Leathard – The Fight for Family Planning: The Development of Family Planning Services in Britain, 1921 – 74 , 1980

13. Lesley Hall, Life and Times of Stella Browne, ibid

14. Edith How-Martyn and Mary Breed – The Birth Control Movement in England, 1930

15. Lesley Hoggart – Feminist Campaigns for |Birth Control and Abortion Rights in Britain, 2003

16. Quoted in R.A. Solloway, *Birth Control and the Population Question in England, 1877 – 1930*, 1982

17. Marie Stopes, *The First Five Thousand: being the first report of the first birth control clinic in the British Empire*, 1924

18. Opening Remarks: The Galton Lecture, Eugenics Review, 38, 1946

19. Deputation to Minister of Health, John Wheatley (A8/10), Wellcome Collection Archives.

20. NEC Minutes BLPES, Minutes of SJC June 1925

21. *The Labour Woman*, October 1927

22. Hansard 1926

23. Hansard ibid

24. Hansard ibid

25. *Report of the Ninth National Conference of Labour Women 1928*

26. LSE Library, Passfield/4/26, LSE website

27. Bondfield, *A Life's Work*, 1948

28. Deputation to Minister of Health, John Wheatley (A8/10)

CHAPTER 2
Work

*"I remember on one occasion when a grocer, the owner of a shop, took a bill, read it, tore it up and stamped on the bits and said: 'Union indeed! Go home and mend your stockings.' **My** stockings were always mended!"*

Margaret Bondfield, *A Life's Work*, 1948

Margaret Bondfield's life was about work, both her own and that of working-class women. Of the female Labour MPs returned during the inter-war years, Margaret Bondfield stands out as a tireless champion of women in paid employment. The formidable Miss Bondfield made women and work her own epic struggle, rising to become the leading woman trade unionist of her day, and later Minster of Labour and the first woman in the Cabinet.

Margaret's personal experience of work mirrored that of many women in the 'female trades' immediately before and after the First World War. As was the case with many bright girls, the young Margaret spent a year as a teacher in her native town of Chard in Somerset. In 1887 at the age of fourteen she travelled to Hove, near Brighton, to become an apprentice assistant in a draper's shop, a post she had been offered by a family friend. Although considered suitable female employment, shop work was gruelling, with long hours and low pay, and the Hove establishment was no exception. The employment's acceptability may well have been due to the requirement at the time that shop girls live in their employers' premises, thus offering female employees a level of safety and protection.

Margaret Bondfield, helped no doubt by her non-conformist faith and ethics that were very much part of her west country upbringing, had a strong sense of the dignity of work. Having absorbed her father's radicalism, Margaret was repelled by what would now be seen as the exploitation of shop workers in the Hove store. 'Living in' effectively made shop work little different from domestic service –

Margaret Bondfield, Britain's first women Cabinet Minister, 1930

on-call all hours with virtually no privacy. The accommodation at Hove was an insanitary dormitory in the roof.

By 1894 Margaret felt the need to move on, deciding to try her luck in London, where she had to search hard for work as it was difficult to come by. When Margaret eventually settled in a job, she discovered that the conditions she thought peculiar to the store in Hove were almost universal. She worked sixty-five hours a week for between £15 and £25 a year, low wages even by the standards of the time.

"The inside knowledge I obtained of the appalling conditions in the homes of women wage-earners turned me into an ardent socialist." [1]

Needing to channel her anger and frustration, the young Margaret joined the National Union of Shop Assistants, Warehousemen and Clerks (NUSAWC) and began contributing to its journal using the pseudonym Grace Dare. Miss Bondfield had found her vocation, a vocation which would eventually take her to the very top of British politics:

> "For the next two years the Union utilized me for platform work to an ever-increasing degree….It was stimulating to discover that I could dominate a rowdy meeting, and reduce it to good order, thanks to the gift of a good voice, stout lungs, and a knowledge of Palgrave's *Chairman's Handbook*." [2]

Slogans such as "Death to the Living-in system", "Abolish fines and deductions", and "Reduce the hours worked in shops" inspired the idealistic young woman.

Rousing rhetoric and committed campaigning were only part of Margaret Bondfield's new life. Margaret was passionately committed to justice, in particular justice for working women. In 1896 she was recruited by the Women's Industrial Council (WIC) to help with an investigation into shop assistant conditions. Working undercover, Margaret's mission was to obtain engagements at various shops at her own discretion and stay just long enough to judge conditions. Starting in high-end shops she descended the scale of the retail world as her references grew shorter. Margaret, in actual fact, ruined her future in the retail profession for the sake of the shop girls who came after her.

In 1901, seventeen years before some, but not all, women were granted the vote, Margaret Bondfield presented evidence on shop reform to the House of Lords select committee on early closing of shops, and to the departmental committee on the Truck Acts seven years later. Ultimately Margaret's evidence was used by Sir John Lubbock as material for four short Shop Assistants' Acts between 1892 and 1899, which made, amongst other things, significant alterations to living-in conditions.

Margaret Bondfield's outstanding dedication and extraordinary determination were rewarded when she was made Assistant Secretary of the Shop Assistants' Union in 1898. Typically, she immersed herself in her work, seeing union membership rise by one thousand during her first year there. Although Bondfield lamented the difficulties in recruiting women workers, other important victories were achieved. In her autobiography Margaret noted that:

> "…on the other hand a small minority of active women had had a great influence in developing the policy of the whole movement. In the Shop Assistants' Union women took an active part in securing legislative safeguards….This was the first Union to work for the regulation of hours by legislation applying equally to its men and women members."[3]

Sadly this enlightened attitude taken by the NUSAWC Shop Workers' Union has received little recognition.

Yet again Margaret paid a heavy price, albeit one she seemed very prepared to make. Having sacrificed her own prospects in the retail trade to improve the conditions of her fellow workers, Margaret Bondfield went on to negate whatever thoughts she may have had about marriage and a family:

> "This concentration [on her work as Union Assistant Secretary] was undisturbed by love affairs. I had seen too much – too early – to have the very least desire to join the pitiful scramble of my workmates….I had no vocation for wifehood or motherhood, but an urge to serve the Union – an urge which developed into a sense of 'oneness with our kind'." [4]

Indeed, one of the most striking things about Margaret Bondfield is her almost total lack of a private life. When she became NUSAWC Assistant Secretary in 1908 she was thirty-five years old, significantly past the ideal marriageable age according to Edwardian convention. The only hint of any romantic relationship during these early years is, perhaps unsurprisingly, with a woman she met in the course of her work. This woman was Mary Macarthur, with whom Margaret formed the first women's general union, the National Federation of Women Workers in 1906. The two women became close colleagues and formed a very strong friendship, perhaps more. In her 1924 biography of Margaret Bondfield, Mary Agnes Hamilton describes the relationship between Bondfield and Macarthur as a "very real romance", though this may only refer to the intensity of the friendship rather than a sexual relationship. Bondfield and Macarthur did, in fact, live together for three years, though this should not be taken at anything more than face value, since then - as now - single people of the same sex would often share a house or apartment, viewing it as a convenient and often temporary arrangement. Even so, there is some evidence that the Bondfield-Macarthur relationship was more than platonic. Bondfield describes her feelings on first meeting Macarthur in adoring terms:

> "It was a dazzling experience for a humdrum official [Bondfield] to find herself treated with the reverence due to an oracle by one whose brilliant gifts and vital energy were even then manifest. So might a pigeon feel if suddenly worshipped by a young eaglet." [5]

When Mary Macarthur died in 1921 Bondfield wrote in her autobiography:

> "The companionship of eighteen years work and play…. - always salted with humour, sweetened by affection, lit by a deep unfailing zest in life that neither labour nor sorrow could dim – was ended." [6]

In 1908 Margaret Bondfield resigned from her Assistant Secretary post with the National Union of Shop Assistants Warehousemen and Clerks to pursue other avenues. Bondfield was by this time a member of the Independent Labour Party, which led her to speak at the Trades Union Congress in 1899 in favour of the creation of the Labour Representation Committee. Such a timely intervention (the Labour Representation Committee was formed a year later) may indicate that Margaret was thinking of a change of direction towards becoming an elected representative.

Margaret, in addition, became leader of the Adult Suffrage Society, and in 1906 helped found the Women's Labour League (WLL). She also renewed her interest in social investigation, undertaking work for the Women's Industrial Council on women's employment and for the Women's Co-operative Guild on maternity and child welfare.

The ardent trade unionist had become the consummate political campaigner. The introduction, from 1914 onwards, of state maternity benefits and improved medical care for mothers and infants owed much to the work carried out by Margaret Bondfield. Yet Bondfield's heart always lay with the trade union movement. Following the establishment of the Standing Joint Committee of Working Women's Organisations (SJC), comprising the National Federation of Women Workers (NFWW), the Women's Trade Union League, the Women's Co-operative Guild and the Women's Labour League in 1912, Margaret resumed full-time office as NFWW Organising Secretary.

Unlike some of her colleagues, Bondfield's stance was always to seek equal status with men rather than a distinctive female position. Interestingly, by the time of the Labour Party's most fundamental reorganisation ever in 1918, Margaret Bondfield appeared to believe that equal status with men was well advanced. She therefore accepted the Women's Labour League conversion into women's sections of the Labour Party, and the merger of the National Federation of Women Workers with what had become the National Union of General and Municipal Workers (NUGMW). Bondfield was appointed NUGMW Chief Women's Officer on the day in 1921 that Mary Macarthur died, fittingly the same day that the National Union of Women Workers ceased to exist as an independent organisation.

Thus Margaret Bondfield, the shop worker born and brought up in rural Somerset, became the leading woman trade unionist of the 1920s. Work was her life and her success was due to her extraordinary capacity for hard graft, her strong intelligence and steely determination, together with her extraordinary public speaking ability. In the pre-television age platform performance was all, and Margaret, small in stature though she was, excelled in this arena. Mary Agnes Hamilton has this to say on one of Bondfield's speeches given in 1918:

> "Here was the right voice: a voice instinctive with command, with the secret power of courageous will…The burning soul within this little, bright-eyed women rouses a responsive chord in any body of people with whom she comes into contact…" [7]

In 1923 Margaret Bondfield became the first woman chair of the Trades Union Congress (TUC), having been elected to its executive in 1918. It was also in 1923 that Margaret began her parliamentary journey to high office, when she was elected as Labour MP for Northampton, one of the first three Labour women returned to the House of Commons that year. Miss Bondfield had reached the very pinnacle of political achievement, and quickly gained recognition for ability and hard work. In her autobiography, Leah Manning, later to become Labour MP for East Islington,

Margaret Bondfield campaigning in Northampton

described 'Maggie' Bondfield as the star of the women members.

Margaret's success was consolidated the following year when she became parliamentary secretary to the Minister of Labour and the first woman to be appointed a Government Minister, thus building on her expertise in the world of work. Defeated in the 1924 election, Bondfield was returned to Parliament for the Wallsend Constituency in a by-election in July 1926. When Labour formed a government after the 1929 General Election, Bondfield was appointed Minister of Labour, Britain's first women Cabinet Minister.

It was by no means plain sailing. Government in 1929, the year of the Wall Street Crash and the beginning of the Great Depression, inevitably proved far tougher than anything Margaret or the Labour Party itself had so far faced. Margaret served two years as Minister of Labour, her work dominated by the question of unemployment

Margaret Bondfield with Ellen Wilkinson and colleagues in 1927

insurance, and the provision of protection for those who lost their jobs. Bondfield found herself in an impossible place. The official Labour Party-TUC position, reflecting the laudable though unrealistic idealism of the time, was to fund more generous benefits from general taxation. Yet the worst economic crisis the world had yet experienced made this impossible.

The country needed strong and inspired leadership during this turbulent period, with the heavy industry which had kept Britain solvent for so long going into decline. It is one of the enduring tragedies of the history of the Labour movement that no-one in this second Labour government, from Prime Minister Ramsey MacDonald down, had a coherent, credible policy to even begin to deal with the economic problems. In retrospect it is hardly surprising that MacDonald felt he could not hang on. However, his subsequent formation of the National Government that included Conservatives proved deeply damaging to the Labour Party, leading to electoral collapse in 1931 when Bondfield herself was a casualty.

Never one to shirk what she perceived as her duty, as Minister of Labour Margaret Bondfield took a robust line on unemployment insurance. On moral as well as financial grounds she believed in a contributory scheme, as opposed to paying out from general taxation, and felt strongly that the insurance fund should not be in debt. Bondfield had, in fact, signed the Blanesburgh Committee report in 1927 (two years before she became minister), which advocated a solvent insurance fund with some restrictions of benefit. She had, inevitably, attracted much criticism from the Labour Party and the TUC for her stand.

Margaret Bondfield with Prime Minister Ramsay MacDonald

Bondfield maintained her position on unemployment insurance after her appointment to the Cabinet, attracting further criticism. From February 1931 her policy was to cut benefit rates. When Ramsay MacDonald adopted the same point of view, proposing the reduction of levels of benefit in August that year, it fatally split the Cabinet. MacDonald then went on to form the National Government. Sadly and inevitably Margaret Bondfield's political reputation collapsed along with MacDonald's Labour Government. Following Labour into opposition she was defeated at Wallsend in the 1931 by-election, never again to return to the House of Commons.

Women at work, their pay and conditions, their livelihoods and their futures, had always been Margaret Bondfield's passion, the cause to which she dedicated her life. Prominent women such as Bondfield who were able and willing to speak out were sorely needed. Once the First World War ended, the impetus for women to act as substitutes for men's jobs also ended, causing a dramatic switch in the portrayal of women workers. In 1915 women were urged to register for emergency war work at the local labour exchange. By 1921 fewer women were in paid employment than in 1911, and those who worked came to be seen as 'parasites', 'blacklegs' and 'limpets' almost overnight. Women, however, wished to continue to earn money. In 1925, one advertisement for 40 women soda-fountain attendants at a weekly wage of £2.10s, produced 8,000 applicants, 6,000 of whom applied personally, prompting the local police to turn up on horseback to disperse them. [8]

Domestic service after the First World War remained a significant employer for women, despite evidence that there was a dramatic fall in young women's participation in this work, which was characterised by low pay, lack of freedom and unregulated hours. According to the 1911 census, 1,271,990 women were employed as domestic indoor servants, and in 1921 this had dropped to 1,148,698, only to rise slightly to 1,332,224 ten years later. There was, however, considerable working-class objection to domestic service, articulated by Labour MP Mr J Jones, who made his views known when he objected to working class women being made flunkeys for women who are far better able to look after their own families. Such strong views however failed to have much effect and the political parties took remarkably similar positions on the issue.

Margaret Bondfield defended domestic service with her customary eloquence, stating in November 1927:

> "I take domestic service to be a highly-skilled profession. I think it has been degraded by the conditions that have been applied to domestic service. There is not a Member in the House who does not depend on domestic service to serve him, feed him, and keep him clean. If it were not for domestic service, we should all die of plague or starvation. I resent most bitterly the stigma and serfdom put upon what ought to be one of the most honoured professions in the country. Until the removal of that stigma, and until you place that work – probably the most skilled and varied job a woman can be asked to do, and calling for the greatest individuality and initiative – in the position it ought to occupy as a well-trained, well-regulated profession, there will always be this difficulty about getting the necessary supply." [9]

Bondfield went on to stress the need for training and to maintain the government grant for women's vocational training, which included a small domestic scheme.

However, lack of specific training was not really where the difficulty lay. Far more problematic was the fact that domestic service was not an insured trade for unemployment benefit, another indication that it was regarded as low status employment, a view strengthened by pitifully low wages. Girls who had some degree of training only earned in the region of ten shillings a week, compared with twelve to fifteen shillings for women agricultural workers at the beginning of the First World War.

To their credit, the Labour Party and the Standing Joint Committee of Working Women's Organisations (SJC), comprising women from the Labour Party and the trade union movement, sought to tackle the problem of domestic service, producing their report on equal pay for equal work and the first steps towards a domestic workers charter in 1930. The recommendations for the charter can at best be described as pragmatic, at worst woolly and lacking anything which could actually be implemented. The report, however, did recognise the need to improve the status of domestic workers and:

> "...to assure the worker the independence and friendly support of her environment associated with the women industrial worker." [10]

The report also argued for the provision of service flats and hoped for the development of a communal domestic help service to assist overburdened working-class mothers.

With the benefit of hindsight it appears that the Labour Party and the SJC were, in actual fact, barking up the wrong tree. Women, on the whole, did not want better domestic service; rather they did not want to do it at all. The figures speak for themselves – from the end of the nineteenth century to 1911, between eleven and thirteen per cent of the female population of England and Wales was employed as domestic servants. By 1931 it was under eight per cent. [11] Women were clearly voting with their feet; young women left the sector altogether, while those who were older increasingly obtained part-time domestic employment that fitted around family responsibilities.

Domestic service was by no means the only issue relating to women's paid employment taken up by the Labour women MPs in the inter-war years. Employment and industrial matters were always high on their agenda. Margaret Bondfield was not alone in gaining her initial experience and early breaks through the trade union movement. Eight of the Labour women MPs between 1923 and 1939 came to Parliament this way, reflecting the early twentieth century Labour Party's union base. The trade union route to becoming a Labour MP was as important for women as for men during this period, and much more difficult for women to access given their differing employment patterns and the obvious discrimination against married women.

Three of the first four Labour women MPs elected in 1923 and 1924 were employed full-time for a trade union prior to entering Parliament. While Margaret

Margaret Bondfield in 1924

Bondfield was the shining example, Dorothy Jewson worked for the National Union of General and Municipal Workers, and Susan Lawrence had close connections with the women's union movement throughout her time in Labour politics. Ellen Wilkinson, returned to the House of Commons in 1924, was a paid organiser with the Amalgamated Union of Co-operative Employees (AUCE). Unusually, Wilkinson retained her post of National Women's Organiser for AUCE, later the Union of Shop, Distributive and Allied Workers, for the rest of her life. Prior to taking up this post in 1915, Ellen spent two years as an organiser with the National Union of Women's Suffrage Societies in Manchester. From 1919 to 1925 she represented the AUCE on four trade boards, cutting back on this work after her election to the House of Commons in 1924.

While Margaret Bondfield's first love was the women's trade union movement, there is no doubt that Ellen Wilkinson was first and foremost a Member of Parliament. Once returned to the House of Commons at the relatively young age of thirty-three, she lost no time in taking up a number of causes dear to her heart, one of the most important being the plight of women who were disallowed unemployment benefit. Speaking in a debate in March 1926, Ellen Wilkinson pointed out that while one in seven men was disallowed benefit, the rate was one in three for women, and the average extended benefit granted to men was twelve weeks but women only had four weeks:

> "…women are being discriminated in this way. If they are single women, they are told that they must live with their relations. If they are married – our Lancashire women are accustomed to earning their living though married – they are told they must live on their husbands." [12]

In the same speech Ellen went on to talk about widows' pensions, specifically those women whose deceased husbands did not have the necessary number of National Insurance stamps to enable their wives to receive pensions. Ellen Wilkinson challenged the official view that such men were not genuinely seeking work as required under the relevant legislation, and passionately made the case for women in such circumstances to receive the full widows' pension. The speech made her reputation as a strong parliamentary performer with an excellent grasp of detail. Soon Ellen was quietly being marked out as ministerial material:

"[Wilkinson was] becoming, unknown to herself, moulded for the Front Bench and eventually for office: she would make a good departmental minister, more efficient and popular than those Labour stateswomen Susan Lawrence and Margaret Bondfield." [13]

However, in 1926 Ellen Wilkinson still had a way to go. In common with every Labour woman MP, she lost her seat in 1931 following Prime Minister Ramsay MacDonald's decision to form an all-party national government. Wilkinson did, however, manage to come back in the 1935 general election as MP for the north-east seat of Jarrow, an area dominated by heavy industry and massively affected by the Great Depression. Ellen identified wholeheartedly with her constituents, becoming one of the leaders of the famous Jarrow March against unemployment in 1936. *The Town that was Murdered*, Wilkinson's moving book on the effects of unemployment and despair on a proud working-class community, was published in 1939.

In 1936, and anticipating the theme of her book, Wilkinson informed the House of Commons that a Jarrow vicar had told her that the young men there were:

"… just like eggshells. They looked all right outside, but when they were faced with the infection and the cold of winter they just cracked like eggshells." [14]

The Town that was Murdered told of Jarrow's suffering, advocating socialism as its saviour. Wilkinson proclaimed monopoly capitalism the problem, not individuals. The economic system was at fault and the remedy was socialism – nationalisation, tax reform and planning. "Jarrow's plight is not a local problem, it is the symptom of a national evil" [15]. In her book Wilkinson articulated the Labour and trade union point of view - state socialism, the moral and philosophical creed of inter-war Labour.

While Ellen Wilkinson was one of the leaders of the Jarrow March, ten years earlier the Labour women MPs appeared to have little input into the 1926 general strike. Women in the Labour Party, however, did take an active, if supporting, role. *The Labour Woman*, the news sheet for Labour Party women, made appeals to the sisterhood to raise money and provide accommodation for the children of the striking miners, reporting on the work of the Women's Committee for the Relief of

Ellen Wilkinson at a Jarrow Marchers' lunch

Miners' Wives and Children. In order to show solidarity and provide more time for this work, the 1926 National Conference of Labour Women was cancelled.

The soaring numbers of men out of work inevitably led to continual reinforcement of the notion that a woman's proper place was in the home, that marriage and motherhood were a woman's ultimate destiny. Official reports reinforced this point of view, sometimes verging on misogyny, with what today would be viewed as unacceptable discrimination against women. The Pilgrim Trust Report *Men Without Work (1938)*, claimed to have observed that:

> "…the girl of 14 seems to drift into the most remunerative employment immediately available, keeping the alternative of marriage always in view and hoping that sooner or later she will be freed from the fulfilment of a function in industry…Her future is not the most important consideration of the moment, and she is readily enticed into any kind of factory or business that will take her, even when she knows the work offered will neither add to her skill nor, in many cases, ensure her steady employment." [16]

Perhaps the greatest act of official anti-women discrimination was the 1932 National Insurance Act, which reduced benefits payable to married women on the extraordinary grounds that their claims exceeded those of single men. By 1935 male contributors received fifteen shillings a week benefit having paid contributions of 4 1/2d, single women twelve shillings a week on contributions of 4d, and married women just ten shillings for the 4d contribution level. Taking a broader view of anti-female discrimination, women's wages remained lower than those paid to men. The Labour Party/Standing Joint Committee of Working Women's Organisations 1930 Report on Equal Pay acknowledged that nothing would change in industry while women's jobs were 'ghettoised' and put into female categories in order to keep women's wages down; for instance, on the railways ninety-five per cent of women were employed at the lowest grade. Even in the professions, women only earned about eighty per cent of the average male salary.

The 1930 Labour Party/SJC Report on Equal Pay for Equal Work and First Steps Towards a Domestic Workers' Charter, also attacked the tendency to categorise jobs into male and female in order to justify lower wages, and challenged the fact that women in the professions earned twenty per cent less than men. The report was totally opposed to the prevailing wisdom that it was not worth training women and noted that where employers had adopted a fairer stance, they had been stymied. For instance, when Woolwich Borough Council paid the same rate for men and women supervising the municipal pools, the expenditure was disallowed by the Government Auditor in 1928 on the grounds that the pay exceeded the market rate. While vague on domestic service, the report did make concrete recommendations on the wider issues – increasing unionisation, securing model conditions in publicly funded employment, and the development of trade boards.

Any meaningful attempt to make women's pay nearer to that received by men seemed a long way off, despite the Labour Party's official view. Yet the Labour women MPs refused to give up. As far back as 1924, Dorothy Jewson had asked the (Labour) Chancellor of the Exchequer whether he would set up a committee to discuss the question of equal pay for equal work for men and women in the Civil Service. Replying on behalf of the Government, William Graham, the Financial Secretary to the Treasury, told the House of Commons:

> "The position, I think, is that we are quite committed to the principle of equality of opportunity, and generally, also, on the question of equality of pay, but, as I view it, this is very largely a practical matter of how soon that can be attained, and the decision in that at the moment the funds cannot be found for this very large expenditure." [17]

While at a theoretical level it was widely agreed that that unequal pay was unjustifiable, the male dominated Labour Party did not think it an issue worth prioritising.

Important though equal pay was as a campaigning principle for the Labour women MPs, the disparity in male/female wage rates did not deter the growing number of women working in offices during the 1920s and 1930s. This was the era of the office girl and the shorthand-typist, one of the most notable developments of the time. Single women were finding employment, often out of necessity as the carnage of the First World War had resulted in many more women than men of marriageable age. In 1901 there were 55,784 commercial women clerks; by 1911 this had risen to 117,057. Ten years later 429,921 women were working as clerks, draughtsmen and typists, and by 1931 there were 579,945. Yet it was often dull, routine work. According to the Report to the National Conference of Labour Women – Women in Offices (1938) "work is so arranged than one girl undertakes one process only", which enabled output to be easily assessed. The Report further described much office work as a blind alley with little scope for promotion:

> "Old prejudices die hard and the idea that women are capable of accepting responsibility…is still strange and unwelcome in many quarters." [18]

Anti-female discrimination, particularly towards married women, raised its ugly head in the increasing enforcement of the marriage bar. To some, the logical conclusion of the post 1918 drive to end women substituting for men's jobs was to prevent married women undertaking paid employment. Largely affecting women in the professions, it was central government that took the lead. Women in the civil service had to resign upon getting married and the London County Council sacked its married women teachers in 1921, despite opposition from the National Union of Teachers. The LCC decision was strongly criticised by Susan Lawrence, who argued that it was unjust and reactionary and "part of a conspiracy to…replace certified women with untrained girls." [19] Perhaps inevitably, the marriage bar became more prevalent as economic conditions worsened. Female employment was a single woman's preserve. According to the 1931 census ninety per cent of married women were "unoccupied"; the figure for single women was thirty per cent.

There was, however, another side to the employment question, namely conditions at the work. Protective legislation, and whether women should be treated differently from men when it came to regulating the workplace, was a matter of considerable internal Labour Party debate. In 1928 Ellen Wilkinson, supported by, amongst others, Margaret Bondfield and Susan Lawrence, brought forward a Bill to regulate conditions in offices, highlighting in particular the problems faced by women in the workplace:

> "…which were never built to accommodate both sexes and where the sanitary conditions and so on are doubtful, even for men and extremely inadequate for women…." [20]

A year earlier Margaret Bondfield had made an impassioned speech in the House of Commons during a debate on a bill calling to end the ban on women working with lead, particularly in paint, and place them on the same footing as men:

Marion Phillips on the beach in Scarborough 1920

"Regulations are not regarded as a sufficient or adequate defence for men, but even if men prefer to go on being poisoned, that is absolutely no argument why women should go on being poisoned until we have discovered some other way of dealing with the subject." [21]

Although Bondfield went on to say white lead should not be allowed in paint under any circumstances, her essential argument was that just because men suffer, women should not automatically be expected to undergo the same privations.

Bondfield's position was, in part, a reflection of her long service in the women's trade union movement. Marion Phillips, her parliamentary colleague from 1929 to 1931 and near contemporary in age, had also come up through the women's organisation in the Labour Party and the trade union movement - one of the eight Labour women MPs between 1923 and 1939 to have risen via the trade unions. Like Bondfield, Phillips had made an enormous contribution to the cause of women and work in her role as Secretary of the Standing Joint Committee of Working Women's Organisations and from 1918 as the Labour Party's first Chief Woman Officer before entering Parliament.

Marion Phillips began her career in politics in 1905 as an employee of Fabian pioneers, and founders of the London School of Economics Sidney and Beatrice Webb. Once that position ended, Phillips then gained a position as a research assistant to the Royal Commission on the Poor Laws on public health, poor-law medical relief and the treatment of destitute children. Phillips was by this time looking to become politically active; in 1907 she joined the Fabian Society, the Independent Labour Party and the Women's Labour League in 1908, becoming a member of its executive committee the following year. In 1909 she also signed up to the non-militant National Union of Women's Suffrage Societies, demonstrating her political acumen by highlighting the way that militancy distracted from democratic discussion and action. Phillips's trade union credentials were sealed when she became organising secretary to the Women's Trade Union League, and in 1911 the Secretary of the Women's Labour League (WLL). Marion Phillips edited the WLL news sheet, given the title of *Labour Woman* in 1913, from its inception to her death.

By all accounts Phillips was not a popular or particularly likeable character, leading the women's activist Katherine Bruce Glasier to say to Ramsay MacDonald:

> "O, if only she could fall in love and mate and marry. But just now she is as hard and cold as glass." [22]

In 1912 Phillips was elected as a Labour councillor in the London Borough of Kensington. Typically she was a hard-working and committed member of the council, pressing for public provision of baby clinics, school meals, improved council housing, employment schemes and the prohibition of sweated labour. During the First World War, Marion Phillips took up duties appropriate to her upwardly mobile career path, becoming a member of the War Emergency Workers' National Committee, the consumers' council of the Ministry of Food and the Central Committee on Women's Training and Employment. During 1917-18 she served on the committee for post-war reconstruction. She also became a member of the advisory committee of London magistrates.

In common with several of the Labour women MPs returned between 1923 and 1945, Marion Phillips was a strong believer in the need for separate women's political organisations, at least until women caught up with men in political experience. In 1918 she edited a volume of essays, *Women and the Labour Party 1918*, which aimed to show "the contribution which the Labour Party has to make upon questions that are peculiarly the concern of women." [23].

Towards the end of the War, Phillips came back to women in the labour movement, becoming Secretary of the Standing Joint Committee of Working Women's Organisations in 1917. In 1918 after the Women's Labour League branches became the Women's Sections of the Labour Party, Marion Phillips took up the newly created post of Labour Party Chief Woman Officer. Phillips had now reached the top of the Labour Party. Nevertheless, her grating personal manner continued to attract scathing comment. In May 1918, Beatrice Webb referred to Phillips' "…insolently critical attitude towards all persons and institutions", her "sharp satirical tongue" and that she was "much disliked by the other leading women in the labour movement". [24] It was only Phillips' ability and outstanding work ethic that allowed her to overcome her unpopularity.

In contrast to today's user friendly politicians, when United States Presidents are judged as much on their presentation as their programme, likeability was not a requirement in the pre-television and mass media age. Phillips, in fact, went on to fulfil her new role with distinction. 2000 Labour Party Women's Sections came into existence within 14 years. Phillips, with some help, put together a practical manual, *Women's Work in the Labour Party*, and ensured that *The Labour Woman* maintained its earnest demeanour, repudiating anything she considered frivolous. The news sheet was firmly aimed at "the sane working women who feels her responsibilities as a citizen and desires to carry them out." [25]

Phillips also carried out the unglamorous organisational work so essential for the nascent Labour Party, while pressing for improved amenities on working-class housing estates – community centres with nurseries, communal kitchens, libraries, concert halls and home help services. Throughout her working life, Phillips sought to emancipate the working-class housewife. As the Labour Party's Chief Woman Officer her overarching aim was to get women to vote for the Party and to encourage women to join it. Moreover, Phillips was not what may be termed a feminist, in that she would always toe the Party line, the most significant demonstration of this being her refusal to support the Labour Women's Conference in their demands for accessible birth control. Phillips always, and with justification, protected her own position within the Labour Party hierarchy, rewarded ultimately with a seat in the House of Commons.

In 1929 Marion Phillips was elected for the double-member seat of Sunderland. She quickly took up the plight of her constituents, badly hit by the depression. Defending annual paid holidays in Parliament in November 1929, Phillips made the point that "the sort of holiday that my constituents in Sunderland get is an involuntary holiday, with either Poor Law relief, unemployment benefit or nothing at all. [26] Phillips, of course, suffered in the 1931 wipe-out, losing Sunderland in the general election of that year. Marion Phillips died the following year in the Empire Nursing Home, Vincent Square, London at the age of fifty-one.

While work was everything for both Margaret Bondfield and Marion Phillips from their earliest years, Leah Manning, nee Perrett, at least enjoyed some kind of youth as a trainee teacher at Homerton College:

> "I won't pretend I was a very serious student. I worked hard at the subjects that interested me, especially those that concerned my training as a teacher, and utterly neglected others. This gave me time for the social side of college life which I enjoyed enormously." [27]

Leah Manning was even more unlucky than Marion Phillips in the 1931 Labour debacle. Leah, another woman who had come up through the trade union ranks in the form of the National Union of Teachers, was returned to the House of Commons in a by-election in February 1931 only to lose her seat in the general election in October. Elected to the Labour Party National Executive Committee in

1930, she also lost that position in 1931. Leah Manning did, however, get back into Parliament in the 1945 Labour landslide for the marginal seat of Epping.

Leah Manning was often described as an educationalist as well as a politician, and unlike Marion Phillips was an engaging woman with a strong sense of humour. Her entry into Homerton Teacher Training College in Cambridge in 1906 began a career in education which she pursued with passion and enjoyment. Leah did, in fact, receive an A teaching mark which meant she could take her pick of the sought-after London teaching posts. She opted instead to stay in Cambridge and teach at New Street slum school where:

> "…the children were so poor, so undernourished, and so apathetic, that it seemed impossible to stroke one spark of interest from them" [28].

As with Margaret Bondfield, work and the union were Leah Manning's life. Having had a daughter in 1918 who died after only three weeks, Leah and husband William seem to have drifted apart. Will was posted to Canada in 1939 and the couple eventually stopped living together. But Leah was no austere workaholic. A left-wing socialist she spoke her mind, calling Mr Hastings Bertram Lees-Smith, Labour President of the Board of Education in 1931:

> "…a man entirely without strength in this controversial matter [raising the school leaving age] and regarded by teachers as a black-leg minister." [29]

The tall and well-built Leah was a strong and effective campaigner and a fiery orator. She was a left-wing socialist whose political outlook was founded on her warm humanitarianism and her love for her fellow men and women and, of course, the young people to whom she dedicated so much of her life.

By the time the final two Labour women MPs who had strong trade union connections reached the House of Commons in the late 1930s, it was no longer mandatory that Labour women MPs be single, despite the tightening of the marriage bar in many professions. Both Agnes Hardie and Jennie Adamson were married, Hardie taking over her husband's seat of Glasgow Springburn on his death in 1937. Adamson was elected in a by-election in Dartford in Kent in 1938.

Agnes Hardie, nee Pettigrew, was born in September 1874 at Barnhill in the Springburn district of Glasgow. Her father, John Pettigrew, was the assistant governor of the Barony poorhouse. Like Margaret Bondfield, Agnes worked as a shop assistant but unlike Bondfield Agnes always regretted that she never had the opportunity of an academic education. Again like Bondfield, Agnes was drawn into the Labour movement. Agnes helped to organise Scottish shoemakers in 1893, which eventually led to her appointment as the first woman full-time organiser with the National Union of Shop Workers. It seems highly likely that Agnes Hardie would have met Margaret Bondfield, and she would certainly have known of her since women at the higher levels of the Labour Party were still few and far between at this time. Agnes Hardie campaigned all her life to improve the conditions of

Agnes Hardie 1937

shop workers and cited her own experience of working twelve hours a day, six days a week:

"I never had a half holiday or Saturday afternoon until I was married" [(30)].

Agnes Hardie was also active in the Independent Labour Party and by 1907 she was being put up as a platform speaker addressing women in Scotland. The division between men and women in Labour politics at the beginning of the twentieth century is again evident. It was, in fact, highly unusual for a women to speak in public at this time; that it was a fact of life for the first Labour women MPs is yet another indication of how brave and special they all were. Hardie was elected ILP member of the Glasgow School Board in 1909, the first female member of the ILP to sit on a public authority board. She also became the first female member of Glasgow Trades Council, helping to organise mill girls in the sewing trades in Bridgeton in Glasgow. In 1918 Agnes was appointed Women's Organiser for the Labour Party in Scotland.

In 1909 Agnes married George Downie Blyth Crookston Hardie, a half-brother of Keir Hardie, the first Labour MP elected in 1892. At the end of 1909 Agnes and George had a son who sadly predeceased both of them. Thirteen years later in 1922, George Hardie was himself returned as Labour MP for Glasgow Springburn. Following the custom at the time, Agnes moved to London after George's election, becoming active in the Ealing and Finchley branches of the Labour Party. On George Hardie's death on 26 July 1937, Agnes inherited his seat, a practice which has happened on and off in politics over the years. She easily defeated her Conservative rival and represented the constituency until 1945, when she decided to stand down. Agnes Hardie died six years later in 1951.

Janet Laurel Adamson, nee Johnston, was another Scottish woman, born in Kilmarnock in May 1882. Janet, known as Jennie, later recalled in Parliament:

"…my mother was left a widow with six young children and the impression left on me by my young life have never been removed by the passage of time" [(31)].

Jennie's mother had taken up dressmaking on the death of her husband, and Jennie had to help her out while still at school. Fortunately perhaps, Jennie also managed to gain some employment as a schoolteacher. In 1902 at the age of twenty, Jennie married William Murdoch Adamson, a pattern maker who was also a trade union activist. Jennie Adamson, unlike some of her female colleagues, had a family

Mrs. Adamson presiding at International Women's Committee, Paris, August 27th 1933

life fairly typical of the time with four children, two sons and two daughters. She joined the Labour Party in 1908 and the Workers' Union, in which her husband was already gaining prominence, in 1912. His union activities required them to move frequently and Jennie herself became involved in union work, notably during the Black Country strike of 1913. By 1921 William Adamson was appointed head of the Workers' Union east midlands division. Jennie and the family followed him to Lincoln where she became involved with the Lincoln Co-operative Society. From 1922 to 1925 Jennie was a poor law guardian, creating a spectacle with her *boots for bairns* campaign, which she launched with a procession of unemployed and their barefoot children. They marched to the workhouse in a line headed by an elephant borrowed from the local circus.

In 1923 William Adamson was elected Member of Parliament for Cannock Chase. The family moved to London where Jennie was able to become more active in politics. She was a strong supporter of the 1926 General Strike, sitting on the women's national strike committee. Jennie was elected to the London Labour Party's executive committee in 1927. The following year she became chair of the influential Standing Joint Committee of Working Women's Organisations and chaired the National Conference of Labour Women in 1928. Jennie Adamson, like virtually all the early female Labour MPs, gained her spurs in the women's labour movement. She went on to be elected to the London County Council in 1928 and remained a member until 1931. She also served on the Labour Party's National Executive Committee (NEC), a far more important body then than it is today, and was elevated to the position of NEC Chair in 1935. Like Susan Lawrence before her, Jennie was elected to the London County Council, a position she held from 1928 to 1931. This allowed her to make important political contacts and gave her the prominence to try for a seat in the House of Commons. However, like many women, she had to wait a long time.

Jennie Adamson became MP for Dartford in a by-election in 1938 on the death of the Conservative Member. Her majority of 4,238 was in large part due to her vociferous opposition to the recently concluded Munich agreement. Her husband was still an MP so they became the House of Commons only married couple. Jennie retired from Parliament in 1946, perhaps because her husband had died the previous year. Jennie Adamson was one of the few early Labour women in the House of Commons who managed to combine her political activity with a successful marriage and family life. In that, she proved a role model for future women in politics.

Two of the Labour women MPs stand out for their professional work. Two female doctors, unusual enough in itself at this time, became Members of Parliament – Dr Ethel Bentham in the 1929 General Election and Dr Edith Summerskill at a by-election in April 1938. Dr Ethel Bentham, elected at the age of sixty-eight to represent East Islington, was an MP for two years until the disastrous 1931 election. She had been in general medical practice since the late 1890s.

Born in London in 1861, Ethel Bentham grew up in Dublin. Visiting the Dublin slums with her mother on charitable missions inspired the young Ethel to become a doctor as a means of helping the poor. She began her training at the London School of Medicine for Women at almost thirty years of age, gaining her certificate in medicine in 1893. She then returned to Dublin, qualifying in midwifery at the Rotunda Hospital for Women, before studying further in Paris and Brussels where she achieved an MD degree in 1895. After a short period working in London hospitals, Ethel Bentham went into general practice in Newcastle upon Tyne.

Bentham moved to London in 1909, living in Holland Park and continuing in general practice. Ethel Bentham now began her involvement in Labour politics. In 1910 she gained a place on the executive committee of the Women's Labour League, chairing the committee regularly. She also held office in the Fabian Society. When the Women's Labour League was absorbed into the Labour Party in 1918, Bentham came top in the ballot for the women's places on the Labour Party National Executive Committee (NEC). She served on the NEC from 1918 -20, 1921 – 26 and from 1928 until her death in 1931. From 1921- 1925 Ethel Bentham was a member of Kensington Borough Council representing Golborne Ward and was, in addition, one of the first cohort of women to serve as magistrates, working mainly in the children's courts, and sat on the Metropolitan Asylums Board.

At the age of sixty-eight, having stood unsuccessfully on three separate occasions, Ethel Bentham was returned as Labour MP for East Islington. She was never a prolific Commons performer during her two years in Parliament, though she did

Ethel Bentham 1931

introduce a bill on married women's nationality in November 1930. She will probably be best remembered for her work on infant welfare prior to entering the House of Commons. In 1911 she was one of the leaders in establishing a pioneering baby clinic in North Kensington as a memorial to Margaret Macdonald and Mary Middleton. As its medical officer, Ethel Bentham underwrote the clinic's expenses and undertook much of the administration. A baby hospital was opened in 1919 to complement the work of the clinic; its surgical ward was named the Ethel Bentham ward after her death.

Dr Edith Summerskill always said that it was going on home visits at a young age with her doctor father, seeing ill-health and poverty first-hand, which made her become a doctor and get involved in politics. Edith Summerskill, born in April 1901 in London, was the youngest daughter of Dr William Summerskill MRCS LRCP and Edith Clara Wilde. Edith qualified as a doctor in 1924 having studied at Kings College and Charing Cross Hospital. Her father, who was obviously a strong influence, was involved in politics as well as his medical practice. Edith claimed her father was a liberal in the tradition of Gladstone, at a time when such radicalism was rare in his profession.

In August 1925 Dr Edith Summerskill married Edward Jeffrey Samuel, whom she had met when a medical student. They formed a long-standing medical practice in north London where Edith's socialist beliefs were made stronger by her continued exposure to ill health and poverty. Many years later, in 1985, Edith Summerskill recalled attending her first confinement as a newly qualified doctor. Shocked at the impoverished home and the undernourishment of the mother whose first child had rickets, she said:

"In that room, that night, I became a socialist" [32]

Summerskill became an early member of the Socialist Medical Association (SMA), founded in 1930 and affiliated to the Labour Party a year later. The SMA started out, and remained, a radical organisation, calling as it did for a socialised health service. Edith came up with the idea of organising social events to raise money and gain publicity for the organisation. Middle class professionals such as Edith Summerskill and the doctors in the Socialist Medical Association were relatively rare in the Labour Party at this time, dominated as it was by male trade unionists. Edith, on the left of the Party during the 1930s, was also a feminist, paying particular attention to women's social and political issues. She was outspoken on the high level of maternal mortality during the 1930s, demanding the interests of the expectant mother be made a priority by the maternity services. Underpinning all the campaigning on health were the fundamental claims for a publicly funded and administered health care service.

Edith also began her career as an elected Labour representative in the 1930s. In 1934 she won a by-election to Middlesex County Council and represented the working-class Green Lanes division of Tottenham until 1941. This victory was important. Labour morale was at a low ebb so local victories such as this were important in boosting Party confidence at a time when locally elected bodies had significant powers and commanded widespread respect and loyalty. Summerskill was also Labour's unsuccessful candidate in a parliamentary by-election in Putney in the same year.

Edith Summerskill really showed what she was made of in the 1935 General Election. Selected to fight the Lancashire seat of Bury, the feminist doctor and well-known proponent of birth control was approached by members of the Roman Catholic clergy, offering their support only if Summerskill promised never to give any women birth control advice. Important though the support of the Catholic Church was in the Bury constituency, Summerskill refused to agree to their demands which resulted in her being denounced from Roman Catholic pulpits on the Sunday preceding the election. Edith lost and saw her treatment as highlighting the difference in the way politics was conducted between the north of England and London.

After Bury, Edith decided to return to her home city. She won West Fulham for Labour in 1938 and was returned in the General Elections of 1945, 1950 and 1951. The constituency was abolished after a boundary review, and from 1955 to 1961 Edith Summerskill was MP for Warrington. She became a minister in Attlee's 1945 Labour Government, a member of the Labour Party National Executive Committee in 1944, and a life peer in 1961.

Of the remaining inter-war Labour women MPs, the best known was Jennie Lee, wife of Aneuran Bevan and much later Minister for the Arts in Harold Wilson's Government. Jennie came from a working-class Scottish background; her father was a miner and also an activist in the Independent Labour Party (ILP). Jennie Lee trained as a teacher at Edinburgh University where she also studied law, gaining an MA, her teacher's certificate and an LLB in 1926. Her working-class political background, coupled with the fact that she was brought up as the 'son' of the family, meant that Jennie was always destined for a life in politics.

Having spent only a short while teaching at Glencraig School, Jennie won the mining seat of North Lanark for the ILP in a by-election in February 1929 and held it in the General Election later that year, albeit with a reduced majority. Aged twenty-four when elected, Jennie Lee is the second youngest women ever returned to the House of Commons, second only to the Northern Irish MP Bernadette Devlin. Jennie has the distinction of becoming an MP even before she was old enough to vote. In the House of Commons the beautiful, gifted and passionate Jennie Lee became part of a high-powered left wing grouping which included Ellen

Jennie Lee on a train in 1931

Wilkinson, Charles Trevelyan, Aneurin Bevan and Frank Wise. As unemployment rose, Miss Lee savagely attacked the policies of the 1929 – 31 Labour Government led by Prime Minster Ramsay MacDonald and his Chancellor Philip Snowden, particularly as they cut benefits to the unemployed. Jennie Lee lost her seat in 1931, as did very other Labour woman MP. When the Independent Labour Party refused to submit to official Labour Party discipline in 1932, Jennie Lee followed them into the wilderness. She fought North Lanark unsuccessfully for the ILP in the 1935 General Election, but did not return to the House of Commons until 1945, having renounced the ILP a year earlier.

Mary Agnes Hamilton (nee Adamson) came from a middle rather than a working-class background, though it was academic rather than prosperous. The daughter of a professor of logic at Owens College (later part of Manchester University) and a teacher at Manchester High School for Girls, Molly, as she was generally

Mary Agnes Hamilton

known, attended Newnham College, Cambridge where she read classics and economics, gaining a first class honours degree in 1904. In 1905 she became assistant to the history professor at University College of South Wales, Cardiff. In 1913 Molly decided to try journalism and joined the Economist where her main interests were women's suffrage and reform of the poor law. She published two books on Greece and Rome and two novels before 1914.

Molly Hamilton was a pacifist who joined the Independent Labour Party and was an original member of the pacifist Union of Democratic Control. In 1916 she joined "Common Sense" as assistant editor, also writing for "War and Peace", and became part of Lady Ottoline Morrell's anti-war group, moving in the literary circle which included D.H. Lawrence, Lytton Strachey, the Woolfs and the Huxleys. By 1918 Molly was a well-known journalist and speaker who was later to write biographies of Margaret Bondfield, Ramsey MacDonald and Mary Macarthur.

Hamilton was returned to the House of Commons for Blackburn in 1929, having served on the Balfour committee on trade and industry from 1924 to 1929. From 1929 to 1931 she was a member of the Royal Commission on the Civil Service. Molly Hamilton became Parliamentary Private Secretary to the Postmaster-general Clement Attlee, who called her one of the ablest women ever to enter the House of Commons. As was the case for every other Labour woman MP, she lost her seat in 1931, never returning to Westminster, and concentrating instead on lecturing and broadcasting.

The women elected as Labour MPs in the 1920s and 30s were a varied group. It is striking that almost all of them had received some post-school education, something which was very rare in the inter-war period as less than three per cent of the population attended university. Higher education was also a middle-class preserve; young working- class women like Ellen Wilkinson who gained university scholarships were extremely few and far between. The women who entered Parliament at this time were therefore intelligent and determined pioneers who paved the way for later generations. Since teaching was one of the few professions women were encouraged to take up, it comes as no surprise that so many of them had a background in education. Likewise, women MPs would have been expected to to show their ability and commitment through work in the Labour Party and the trade unions. It was, however, a tragedy for women's representation in the Labour Party that every single one of them lost her seat in 1931, and that it later proved so difficult for women to be elected as Labour MPs between 1931 and the establishment of the war-time coalition in 1940.

The educational backgrounds and their removal from their roots when they became MPs is very striking when seen in the context of the employment of working-class women undertaken at this time. In her biography of Margaret Bondfield, Mary Agnes Hamilton comments on the appalling conditions of women's factory work and the failure of employers to honour commitments imposed by the Factory Acts. Women's work was also badly paid, to such an extent that an editorial in *The Labour Woman* in March 1923 commented that women's wages were falling relative to those before the First World War, and that the minimums set by the Board of Trade were poorly enforced.

At a time when the term working-class had real meaning, not all of the early Labour women MPs could be so described. Yet, on the whole they represented their constituents well; suffering with them as the Great Depression took hold and they all lost their seats in the 1931 general election. Without a doubt they were all true pioneers who triumphed in spite of adversity.

References:

1. Margaret Bondfield "A Life's Work", 1948

2. Bondfield, ibid

3. Bondfield, ibid

4. Bondfield, ibid

5. Mary Agnes Hamilton, "Margaret Bondfield", 1924

6. Hamilton, ibid

7. Hamilton, ibid

8. Briar, "Working for Women? Gendered Work and Welfare Politics in Twentieth century Britain", 1997

9. Hansard 1927

10. Labour Party/SJC Report on Equal Pay for Equal Work and First Steps Towards a Domestic Workers' Charter 1930

11. Joanna Bourke, BBC History, updated 3.3.11

12. Hansard 1926

13. Webb Diaries, 1924-1933

14. Hansard 1936

15. Wilkinson, The Town that was Murdered, 1939

16. Pilgrim Trust, Men Without Work, 1938

17. Hansard 1924

18. Report to the National Conference of Labour Women – Women in Offices (1936)

19. Report to the National Conference of Labour Women ibid

20. Hansard 1928

21. Hansard 1927

22. TNA:PRO, Ramsey MacDonald MSS, 1157/18

23. Marion Phillips, Women and the Labour Party, 1918

24. Diary of Beatrice Webb, 3, 1918

25. *The Labour Woman*, 1920

26. Hansard 1929

27. Leah Manning, "*A Life in Education*", 1970

28. Manning "A Life in Education" ibid

29. Manning "A Life in Education" ibid

30. Hansard 1939

31. Hansard 1942

32. Strangers in the House, Radio 4, 10 Nov 1984

CHAPTER 3
Welfare

Give the Young Couple a chance to start Married Life happily with a house to themselves – That's Labour's Policy.

Poster for Susan Lawrence public meeting, June 1928

Although all the early Labour women MPs were passionately interested in welfare in its broadest sense, three of them – Susan Lawrence, Edith Summerskill and Marion Phillips - took a particular lead in this area. Action on behalf of the working-class and the very poor was indeed sorely needed during the inter-war years and particularly after the 1929 Wall Street Crash and the subsequent Great Depression. The trend towards declining levels of poverty after the First World War changed following the wide-ranging unemployment in the 1930s, when the primary wage earner was unemployed in an astonishing twenty-five percent of households [1]. To put these numbers into context, the equivalent unemployment levels during the economic slump in the mid-1990s were around nineteen percent, an estimated three quarters of whom were deemed below the poverty line. [2]

Susan Lawrence at The Ministry of Health

Susan Lawrence, appointed Parliamentary Secretary to the Ministry of Health in 1929, was at first sight an unlikely champion of the unemployed, the poor and the dispossessed. Hailing from a well-off middle-class family, Miss Lawrence had won a scholarship to study pure mathematics at University College London and had gone on to study at Newnham College, Cambridge. In 1930 Ellen Wilkinson, at the time Susan Lawrence's Parliamentary Private Secretary, described her thus:

> "[She] is the real bluestocking of our age. Not the old-maidish horror of
> the silly suffragette cartoons, but 'bluestocking' as the eighteenth century Dr
> Johnson knew them, women of wit as well as learning......Tall, cold, severe,
> plainly dressed, at first when she rose to speak the House prepared for the
> worst. Then they glimpsed the real Susan, the woman of delicate humour, of
> a merciless wit, of a logic they had believed only masculine, of a mind which
> drank in facts as some men drink whisky." [3]

The Labour women MPs were never on their own when they thought about and dealt with the huge welfare issues of the time. Women in the Labour Party and numerous women's groups across the country were becoming increasingly more effective as pressure groups and lobbyists. Despite not being recognized as head of the household, women from poorer families almost always took full responsibility for the home and taking care of the children and older family members. Before the age of the nuclear family and full welfare 'safety net' women were very much the carers as well as homemakers. There were, indeed, individual women who took up welfare issues in their local communities. One such was Hannah Mitchell, a staunchly feminist Labour Councillor, who made a stand for communal facilities:

> "…pressed for the provision of public washhouses in every district. Mrs
> Mitchell would go as far as to omit wash boilers and ovens too - from all
> future Corporation Estates, so that communal arrangements for cooking as well
> as washing may become a matter of course." [4]

Mitchell joined the Labour Party during the First World War and, while she still struggled with aspects of inequality such as pay rates, felt she had found a place where she was welcomed as an equal. She had attended school for only two weeks and tasted the bitterness of gender inequality when tasked with household chores while her brothers entertained themselves reading or playing games. This, together with a violent mother, drove Hannah away from the family home as a teenager. With such a challenging history and resolute attitude, Mitchell strove to improve society for others through the Labour Party and later as a councillor - and all of this with her sense of humour intact:

> "As soon as I was elected to the Council, I found I had to devote several
> days a week to the work, and once more the tyranny of meals asserted itself,
> for strange to say, even when men are willing for their wives to take on

public work, they never seem to understand that this cannot be done between mealtimes." [5]

Marion Phillips, together with Averil Sanderson-Furniss, Secretary to the Labour Party's Women's Housing Committee and Member of the Housing Council of the Ministry of Health, co-authored a consultative leaflet asking how people would like their homes to be. Sold in 1917-18 at a price of 1s 6d (7.5p in today's currency), the leaflet found its way to over fifty thousand people covering diverse viewpoints: trades unions, cooperatives, adult schools, social workers, women's guilds, and others. There are no records of exactly how many responses were received, but the claim was for "a very large number" of replies. The majority of the data was gathered by holding or attending existing meetings scheduled by special interest groups and discussing the issues based on a set of questions. These covered practical elements such as the best location for certain rooms; should the bath be upstairs or downstairs; which standard fittings or facilities should be included; and what challenges did people experience with current home layouts. Phillips, Sanderson-Furniss and others also asked questions about community areas such as the possibility of a shared garden. The extensive results of this endeavour were then published in 1919 in the book *The Working Woman's House*. The illustrated book included five chapters. The first covered the perspective of the woman of the house; the second the layout of the house; chapter three explored co-operative facilities and was strongly against such arrangements; chapter four looked at the overall environment and the benefits of well thought through town planning; and finally chapter five addressed the impact on women of the 1919 Housing Act.

The opening lines of the book immediately and clearly set out that what was to follow was an opinion that acknowledged the times in which it had been written, but that it also sought to be taken very seriously indeed:

"For many generations, and with special emphasis in the last fifty years, we have been told that woman's place is in the home. If women are to accept this position, they must also claim a right to have that home built according their desires."

The Women's Labour League, an important and influential group formed in 1906 and later to become the Women's Section of the Labour Party, joined the voices of Phillips and Sanderson-Furniss in 1918 in an article in *The Labour Woman*, stating:

"The working woman spends most of her time in her home, and yet she has nothing to do with its planning. It is time this state of affairs ended. After the war there will be urgent need of a million new houses and as great a need for the remodelling of those we have. The working woman with a home of her own will be a voter. Let her first effort of citizenship be to improve this home."

The pervading theme of the day was to create homes that were 'fit for heroes to live in' following a severe post-WW1 housing shortage and a need to invest in new developments. Taking advantage of the zeitgeist, Phillips and Sanderson-Furniss emphasised that for the wealthy it would go without saying that both the man and woman would be consulted by an architect when laying out plans, but the same opportunity would never normally be afforded a working woman.

The book summarised its perspective by stating that a home should not merely be a roof over one's head, it should be a "pleasure to live in". It also considered factors such as sufficient space and natural light, appropriate facilities for cooking, bathing and a rarely recognised need for socialising. There was a great deal of ingenuity in the ideas proposed. For instance, building a block of four houses where the number of bedrooms could be flexible and meet specific household needs by way of locking or unlocking adjoining rooms. In this way, a family with four children could take advantage of space unwanted by an older couple with no dependants. Much was made of the need to limit dust-collecting surfaces, including a suggestion to include a bedroom cupboard in the building plans to avoid the need to purchase an expensive wardrobe, but most importantly to limit the need for dusting such a lumbering beast.

As a method of accessing the public's passion and creativity for this issue, the Daily Mail ran a competition in May 1919 seeking new ideas for housing design. One of the winning submissions provided a means of making spaces adaptable to different family needs. By employing a sliding partition in the main room of the house, the family could then create a separate parlour and living room or a single, larger space. [6]

The chapter on the practical needs of the interior of the home concludes with a wonderful statement that is just as relevant for any homemaker (male or female) today as it was then:

> "If reconstruction is to be a spiritual force, if indeed it is to mean anything more than a mere name, it must surely find its expression in the names of the people. That this end may be attained a woman must be set free to develop her own personality. Her work must be done under such conditions that it may be enjoyable and stimulating. She must have time, not only to feed and clothe her children, but to train their minds and to build up character. She must, in short, be given every opportunity to lead a wider life, and leisure to live that life to the full. Then, and not till then, will she be enabled to take her rightful place in the community and to become the true homemaker."

Sadly, this intelligently collected, collated and presented insight into what would make for a practical and homely household was largely ignored. Statements printed in the pages of *The Labour Woman* indicated the strong feelings of people were overlooked and "cold-shouldered", and as a direct result Phillips and Sanderson-Furniss resigned from the Woman's Housing Committee, specifically accusing then Liberal Minister for Health, Viscount Christopher Addison, of reneging on his commitment to consult on this important issue. In September 1921 the following was published in *The Labour Woman*:

"Labour women must be bitterly disappointed at the way in which their high hopes that the new houses would be built on comfortable labour-saving lines have been destroyed. Though the reports of women, which were accepted by the Ministry of Health, contained many fine ideas as to house planning, the present rage for economy is cutting down all these to the barest minimum, and the new houses being built are exceedingly disappointing." [7]

There were a number of housing acts passed between the wars and reflecting a time of great change in Britain. The first, the Addison Housing and Planning Act of 1919, provided for the building of half a million local authority owned houses for rent. Sadly, funding was not fully dispensed and only two hundred and thirteen thousand houses were ultimately built. The real significance of this Act was that it was the start of large-scale council housing provision. It was deeply unfortunate that the majority of the poor were unable to afford the rents. Matters worsened when in 1923 the Conservative Minister of Health (and by extension housing), Neville Chamberlain, introduced a new Housing Act which essentially overturned the efforts of the former Liberal Government in developing social housing. This Chamberlain Act cut local authority budgets and looked instead to encourage private ownership. However, this in turn was quickly reversed by Labour's first Government with the 1924 Wheatley Housing Act. Named after the new Minister for Health, John Wheatley, this Act was asserted to be the most important legislation passed by the new Government, despite their minority status at the time. The Act once again increased budgets for local authorities for the building of social housing. This resulted in just over half a million new homes by 1933. Those who opposed continuing investment claimed that the poorer members of society were unable to benefit as they could not afford the rent.

Sadly Wheatley did not see fit to involve his female party colleges in the formation of this Housing Act. Maybe, given his background as a miner and publican and his strong Catholic beliefs, it was a step too far and he was not yet ready to accept that women would have anything valuable to add to the debate. This was indeed unfortunate, given the excellent ideas produced by the Phillips/Sanderson-Furniss consultation.

The effects of the Wheatley Act stayed in place until the Conservative-dominant coalition Government abolished it in 1933. They, in addition, reversed the policy introduced by the 1930 Greenwood Housing Act, also under the Labour Government. This Act provided subsidies for, and compelled local authorities to, clear slums, rehousing the tenants as necessary, thereby building on the measures contained in theWheatley Act.

There is no mention of the involvement of women politicians in the development of each new bill. Those members of society held responsible for the household were not deemed knowledgeable enough to be consulted on any of the practical aspects of creating a nurturing and healthy home. Marion Phillips and Averil Sanderson-Furniss's in-depth exposé of the views of women on their dwellings, which was ultimately ignored by policy-makers, was the only time a woman's perspective was sought in such a fundamental area of society. Put into place by a Labour government, the background work on the 1930 Greenwood Act could perhaps have involved the views of women, especially since Labour women had in the past expressed strong views on housing and how they would like to live. However, the time appears to have been quite simply not right for what would have been perceived as a radical departure from the accepted norms.

Despite what can only be described as marginalisation, there were still those who sought to be the voice of the silent majority. Shena Simon, originally a Liberal MP who switched to Labour in 1935, was instrumental in setting up the Wythenshawe Project. Simon sat on - and later chaired - a special committee with oversight of a development opportunity to be built on land donated to the City of Manchester by Simon's husband Ernest. The committee, established in 1928, was formed to develop a modern suburb that would be a model of municipal housing. Simon, who established her feminist credentials with her active support for the female suffrage campaign, had once refused to attend a formal function for a medical institute that had no women on the board or as part of its medical staff. Better known for her work on education than housing, she is commemorated by Shena Simon College in Manchester.

Although the Wythenshawe houses themselves were laudably well equipped, there were some planning issues that had been overlooked. For instance the nearest shops were over a mile away on a route that at various points had no road. There was also no local clinic, and no green space where children could play. Such inadequacies still existed after World War II. The selection process for being allotted one of the houses was rigorous, with the local authority sometimes insisting on inspecting the homes of possible tenants to assess suitability. Monitoring continued after tenants had taken occupation of the new premises and there are stories of people being taken to court for failing to appropriately maintain their home. Rent on the properties was relatively expensive at around 13 to 15 shillings per week from an average salary of £3. Ernest Simon claimed this was affordable for those with a sound grasp on home economics and a willingness to perhaps sacrifice certain luxuries in return for the benefits offered by Wythenshawe.

Despite the challenges, Wythenshawe residents were proud of their estate and there was significant investment by the residents both in terms of time and money to keep improving it year on year. Notable for being the largest council estate in Europe, Wythenshawe was at the time viewed as the boldest scheme that any municipality had yet embarked upon. The local Cooperative Woman's Guild summed up that dream by saying it was:

"…the world of the future - a world where men and women workers shall be decently housed and served, where the health and safety of little children are of paramount importance, and where work and leisure may be enjoyed to the full." [8]

It was not until 1942 that another of the first Labour women MPs, in addition to Marion Philips, took a prominent interest in housing. Margaret Bondfield, by now no longer an MP, wrote to Mr Simon of the Housing Department (Ministry of Health) in September 1942 on behalf of the Women's Group on Public Welfare (of which she was chairman), stating that they were "entirely in agreement with the Ministry as to the need for some machinery in obtaining the views of women on a matter which concerns them deeply since the house is largely their workshop." As a result of Bondfield's intercession, a number of working class housewives were appointed to the Dudley Committee, one of whose tasks was to consider the design of homes to be built after World War II.

This was clearly a key area of interest for Bondfield as is evidenced by a speech she made in the House of Commons in March 1923 on the plight of the housewife:

"On the last occasion on which I went with a deputation to the Ministry of Labour, we discussed very frankly, and very fully, the women's trades, trade by trade…We had, however, to point out that there was the one great occupation of women in this country, the one great occupation which has been severely hit by the War, and that was the occupation of home-making. I do not mean domestic service. I mean the great work of all housewives in the country in making the home, and in developing that home life which has been the backbone and mainstay of this country." [9]

Bondfield went on to state her strong opposition to the provisions of a new scheme to help unemployed young women who were unable to obtain a home. The new scheme, which had much in common with national service, required such women to receive home training if they agreed to a domestic service post once training was complete. In the end the government decided not to go ahead with this measure.

In their book, *Women and the making of built space in England*, Elizabeth Darling and Lesley Whitworth identified the area of housing and welfare as another where women MPs of the time were concerned about being publicly supportive and thereby risking marginalising it as a women's issue. To do so would more than likely have moved housing, building design and associated concerns down the policy priority list. [10] As with birth control, the first Labour women MPs were torn between their heads and their hearts and what was politically expedient. In 1942 Margaret Bondfield chose her heart, a position which may have been made easier because she was no longer a MP, not to mention that, since Britain was in the middle of a world war, domestic policy was lower down the pecking order.

An astonishing thirty-one percent of housing built between the wars was owned by the local authorities. However, because rents were high, access to council housing was not necessarily the dream families hoped it would be. A survey in Stockton revealed that the death rate in council houses was higher than that in the slum areas due to a poor diet, presumably because the majority of income was spent on rent, not food. [11] This problem was later addressed in the Greenwood Housing Act which prompted the introduction of means-tested, tiered rates. The key difference in opinion between male and female politicians on the issue of housing essentially came down to quantity versus quality. Where men celebrated the creation of new buildings, women focused on whether those buildings could, or would, become viable homes that were designed for efficiency and offered a nurturing environment. The creation of walls, floors and roofs was all very well, but access to adequate shops, education centres and areas in which children could play were factors that were too often overlooked.

The challenge of 'women's issues' as a limiting factor on politics impacted on a particularly active and focused pressure group in an interesting way. The Glasgow Women's Housing Association was formed in 1914 specifically to lobby on housing reform. Despite being featured in the local Independent Labour Party newspaper, *Forward*, and congratulated on its views on the rent problems experienced in Glasgow, the GWHA was largely ignored. In 1916, in an effort to shift the perspective from this being purely a woman's issue to one of more general import, the Glasgow Women's Housing Association made a subtle yet significant change in their title to the Glasgow Workers' Housing Association. [12] The GWHA was instrumental in orchestrating the Glasgow rent strikes in 1915.

Sylvia Pankhurst had raised the notion of withholding rent as a means by which women could assert their rights to vote under the banner of "No Vote, No Rent". The momentum gained in 1913 in support of this campaign was disrupted with the start of World War I, but the idea of there being power in withholding rent was not forgotten. These tactics were adopted initially in 1915 by a small group of women led by Mary Barbour in Govan. Mary's introduction to politics came after she married and became active in the Kenning Park Co-operative Guild. She later joined the Independent Labour Party and further developed her political experience in campaigns such as the Socialist Sunday School movement. Mary herself was a working-class housewife and so immediately gained credibility with her peers who supported her efforts to restrict access to eviction officers and others who tried to otherwise recover the missing rent.

News of Mary's success spread to other affected parts of Glasgow and her tactics were adopted with equal effectiveness. News was released of their activities and there was a major public demonstration against the next rises. On 17 November 1915, thousands of women gathered in Glasgow. They were supported by shipyard and other workers and together they marched to the Glasgow Sheriff's Office in the city centre.

As a direct result of the tenacity of one woman, and the support she gathered, the Rent Restrictions Act was quickly passed by Lloyd-George's Government. The Act made provision for improving the legal rights of renters across the UK.

Spurred on by such successes, Mary Barbour continued her political activities by winning the post of Glasgow's first Labour woman councillor on the Town Council. Mary put her energies into campaigning for numerous home and family orientated changes, including free milk for schoolchildren, home helps, wash houses and even pensions for mothers. As one of the few women politicians willing to vocally support the contentious issue of birth control, Mary championed the opening of Glasgow's first family planning clinic and took a lead role as Chair to ensure it was financially stable enough to provide medical support. Mary served on a total of eight committees focused on elements of health and welfare during her time as a Labour Councillor, until she retired in 1931. [13]

Included in campaigns for the welfare of women and families were issues about a woman's right to work. However, campaigns on women and work were not principally about the right to work in and of itself. The perspective was on the benefits to a household of the additional income, such as preventing infant mortality and improving diet and health.

One of the unforeseen challenges towards the end of World War I was a significant number of women who had been trained in important areas such as munitions. These trades, prioritised to support the war effort, meant that many women were not seen to be well enough trained in domestic skills. Naturally this was not a popular perception amongst the women concerned, who were perfectly comfortable with their new-found skills and did not want to take what they perceived to be a step back from holding such important jobs. The Queen's Work for Women Fund (which later became the Central Committee for Women's Employment) saw itself as one of the main channels for in re-educating women in the art of home making. This was underpinned by a need to increase the population to its pre-war numbers and ensure the shortfall would be compensated for in the near future. The first 'National Baby Week' was held in 1916. The debate was still at the forefront of political issues in 1918 when Mary Macarthur stated in an election campaign leaflet that "the great force in politics is going to be the baby."

Additionally at this time, specialist understanding of modern medicine took a significant step forward. This included the area of bacteriology and the role cleanliness played in healthcare. Maternity wards became regular sights in cottage hospitals through the 1920s and 1930s, as a result of the 1918 Maternity and Child Welfare and Midwives Acts. At the same time appropriate home support was provided to women after giving birth and the latter enabled local authorities to financially back the training of midwives. Both of these Acts were important steps in recognising a woman's needs during - and immediately after - childbirth. In addition to the more widespread awareness and usage of birth control, these two key changes in 1918 played an important part in the reduction in child mortality rates during the inter-war years.

The period between the wars was a vitally important time for health care and provision in Britain. The Fabians first made health a political subject when Beatrice Webb and George Lansbury first spelled out the need for state medical service in

Dr Edith Summerskill (third left) with colleagues 1939

1909. The State Medical Service Association SMSA was formed in 1910 by the Liverpool physician Dr Benjamin Moore, who was probably the first person to use the term National Health Service. In 1930 the SMSA was replaced by the Socialist Medical Association, and soon one of its leading lights was Dr Edith Summerskill, General Practitioner and one time Labour MP.

A Ministry of Health having been created by Dr Christopher (Viscount) Addison in 1918 at the end of the First World War, there was soon an acceptance within government that an extended organization was needed giving general availability of services, complete with health centres, distributed according to the needs of the community. Susan Lawrence was appointed Parliamentary Secretary in this Ministry in 1929 following the formation of the second minority Labour administration. Meanwhile health policy continued to develop, and the Socialist Medical Association (SMA) was formed in 1930. Its president, Mr Somerville Hastings, set out the SMA's principles for a new type of medical service at the AGM in May 1931. These were:

1. That it should be preventative, with no economic barrier between doctor and patient, and all citizens to have a right to hospital care

2. The team not the individual, was to be the keynote, with the general practitioner a member of the team

3. There should be a choice of doctor for the patient, and professional freedom for the doctor

4. The service was to operate from health centres, these to include a dental and industrial service, with visits from hospital consultants

5. Hospital consultants would also consult general practitioners in the patients' homes, as in our present domiciliary visits

The SMA, itself affiliated to the Labour Party in 1934, was soon sending people and resources for the Republican forces in Spain. The Association was also deeply concerned, amongst other things, about the almost total separation of GPs and hospital services. The idea of a National Health Service, eventually created by Health Minister Aneurin Bevan in 1948, emerged from these and other strands of thought. [14]

Despite these medical advances, and the efforts of organisations such as the Queen's Work for Women Fund, post-natal support for working mothers and welfare for women in general was severely limited. And where it was provided it was often seen as an intrusion rather than support. As Mary Macarthur said in 1918:

"There is no word in the English language more hated among the women workers today than that of welfare…The workers can look after much for themselves which welfare workers undertake to do. They object to being lectured on their dress…They object to being visited in their homes and they object to organisation of amusements and so on as to counter attractions to their meetings." [15]

It is also unfortunately true that a view arose amongst medical and welfare officers that working-class mothers were feckless and uncaring. There certainly were those in official positions who claimed that many poor parents allowed their children to die so they could claim the insurance money and that this meant that mothers did not love their children. With attitudes such as these, it is easy to see why 'welfare' became something of a swear word in working class society. [16]

Support for families, either in money or in kind, was seen as one way of alleviating poverty, although such a demand met with huge resistance from male trade unions who felt that such a payment would lead to working men's wages being cut. In 1922 the Labour establishment, both in the Party and in the TUC, felt that family support, at this stage only the provision of free boots and clothing rather than a monetary allowance, would not be appropriate given the economic climate. Women should essentially be grateful for whatever they were offered. Ellen Wilkinson, Margaret Bondfield, Dorothy Jewson and Jennie Lee supported the 'no' campaign at the 1922 Labour women's conference on the grounds that the way the topic was positioned implied women were incapable of managing their own affairs. Such designation of funds was very much seen as 'welfare' in the worst, nannying terms, and the group instead campaigned for an allocation much like a regular wage that could be budgeted for and spent as deemed most appropriate by each woman. It was not until 1926 that the Labour establishment stopped seeing this as merely a woman's issue and agreed to seriously consider the options via a national joint committee of the TUC and Labour Party.

The joint committee split in 1928 when it failed to reach consensus on a way forward. Eleven of the committee members supported the Independent Labour Party's proposal to issue five shillings per child. Twelve members however opposed, stating that it would be too expensive a proposition. Marion Phillips tried - and failed - to broker a compromise position which would extend the maternity allowance for a further two years and include the provision of free nursery care.

The issue of the need for boots and clothing did not go away, however, and in December 1928 an emergency meeting held by the Standing Joint Committee on Working Women's Organisations discussed the 'Boots for Bairns' Bill. The Bill recognised that thousands of children were unable to attend school as they had no suitable footwear. The Committee endorsed the Bill and "should recommend to Parliamentary Labour Party that the bill be introduced to give full powers to Education and Public Health Authorities to provide boots for children."

The debate on family allowance then completely disappeared from the Labour Party agenda in 1929 after majority and minority reports were published by the NEC. During a debate on family allowances at the 1929 conference Arthur Henderson MP, one of the Labour Party's most respected figures, voiced the concerns of many, stating the Party could not afford to split on any single area of social reform:

> "We have enough to do to improve social services in areas agreed upon so we should leave the question of family allowances which appears to divide the labour movement into industrial and political sides." [17]

By 1931 there was still no solution and the plight of women was no easier. Stories were common of women in very poor health. As the only wage earner, it was important a woman's husband received sufficient nutrition to continue to work, and no woman would feed herself before her children. So, placed as she was at the end of the queue, it was often the wife and mother who went without.

Odd snobberies built up around the provision of family allowances. One such was put forward by the Prince of Wales Fund which opted not to provide relief to otherwise deserving, albeit unmarried, mothers in case otherwise 'respectable' women would be outraged. A delegation to the Executive of the Prince of Wales Fund, led by Margaret Llewelyn Davies and Margaret Bondfield on behalf of the Women's Co-operative Guild explained that the WCG:

> "… chiefly composed of respectable married women… entirely repudiated that statement and reminded them that every time a woman fell, a man fell also."

Back in 1920, the issue of male pride was posited as a good reason why family allowances would create gender dissatisfaction and emasculation of the husband. Rhys Davies, a trade union delegate to the Labour Party's 1920 conference declared:

"…instead of the working man getting his wages at the factory pay office or colliers pay office, his wife would draw his wage for him at the Post Office."

This perspective was recalled ten years later at the 1930 conference, this time positioned rather differently:

"[This insult] based on the false assumption that the average working-class father was devoid of feelings of responsibility for his wife and children and a confession that the married man could not, either by personal qualities or by trade union organisation, secure an adequate income to maintain himself and his family."

Unfortunately, this rather more enlightened view shared in 1930 was not universal. In a letter to *The Labour Woman*, Labour MP Mr Sommerville Hastings proved provocative in his statement, prompting many angry women to reply that they had the knowledge, just not the money. Sommerville Hastings's letter read:

"…working class women don't have the requisite knowledge to spend an allowance in the right way. They would spend the money in private enterprise on unadulterated food."

A completely contradictory viewpoint than that offered by the Prince of Wales Fund came from Rowntree and a study of working class families in York. Rowntree came out strongly for family allowances, stating in *The Human Needs of Labour* (1939) that:

"…it will be generally admitted that in determining minimum wages no allowance should be made for such precarious sources of income. A woman with a large family has neither time nor strength to do more than to attend to her household duties."

Another significant issue regularly debated by women's interest groups was that of widows' pensions, a cause vigorously espoused by Ellen Wilkinson. The Standing Joint Committee on Working Women's Organisations held an emergency meeting in April of 1925 in response to proposals on widow's pensions. The outcome of this meeting was the production of a circular stating:

"This conference of Labour women protests against proposals to establish widow's pensions on a contributory basis and to transform the whole burden of Old Age Pensions by successive stages to the same system. It declares that the burden of these large insurance payments cannot be met by the workforce without seriously lessening the scanty provision for food and other necessities." [18]

Naturally the Committee was not opposed to the principle of widows' pensions; instead they felt the proposals were inadequate. There were of limited scope and fully omitted any provision for women with an injured - or otherwise incapacitated - husband. In this instance their comments were heeded and the Widows Pensions Bill was passed by the Conservative Government in 1925, including a provision for women whose husbands were incapacitated or absent.

The Standing Joint Committee also debated the thorny issue of abortion. The first mention of abortion reform appears in minutes from a meeting held on 13 December 1934, and continues to be discussed through 1937 when the first indication of any meaningful action is indicated. However that action is merely the collection of more information and medical insight:

> "...reported the correspondence she had had with the Abortion Law
> Reform Association and that she had received further reductions from several
> Women's Sections asking that evidence be collected. It was agreed that the
> secretary should obtain further information as to the objects and aims of
> the Abortion Law Reform Association, discuss the whole matter with Miss
> Lawrence and Mr Greenwood and report further."

Arguments promoting the need for welfare and family support only really seemed to be taken seriously when they were linked directly to the welfare of children. In 1925, the Family Endowment Society presented evidence to the Royal Commission on the coal industry, demonstrating that sixty-six percent of miners' children existed below subsistence level. It was through positions such as these that public and political attention could be captured and focused on improvements to the home that would lessen the family's dependence on the main breadwinner.

In 1934 these tactics were still employed, for instance by the 1934 Children's Minimum Council which was focused on the need to increase unemployment benefits as well as the provision of free milk. To gain Parliament's support they heavily depended on the link between child welfare and the future of society in the UK. In this case, however, the argument was unsuccessful. The Board of Education claimed they could not accept the argument as it would essentially declare the Government's Unemployment Bill insufficient which was something it was not prepared to do.

It was not until the second half of the 1930s that change started to seem possible, the catalyst being the findings of a report in 1937 produced by the Unemployment Assistant Board. The report demonstrated for the first time that six percent of male workers were financially better off claiming unemployment benefits than they would be working. This was largely due to low wages and large families. Such findings prompted responses such as the following from Lady Rhys Williams:

> "It is so much better to uphold the dignity of the home by putting the
> necessary money into the hands of the mother, than by teaching the children to
> look outside the home for all the good things in life." [19]

Looking further afield, a family allowance system was introduced in some other countries as a means of supporting the poorer elements of the population after the First World War. It was then phased out once the immediate need was addressed. For instance, in France a subsidy scheme was introduced to benefit around four million workers, many of whom were miners. The impact included a positive movement in child mortality rates as families were able to properly feed themselves. Naturally other factors came into play, but it was felt the subsidy played an important part in such families achieving a reasonable living standard.

Belgium's system benefitted families with children up to the age of twenty-one and was paid not by the state but by the producers that supplied goods to the state. This policy was pro-birth, particularly as it included an incremental increase in the allowance based on the number of children per family. [20]

A system of allowances for women married to army officers had been tried out during the First World War. It was offered at various stages by charities and the state, but in all cases was highly dependent on a subjective assessment of a woman's moral fortitude. Domestic morality was measured essentially on two things: alcohol consumption levels and evidence of infidelity, and in many thousands of instances led to benefits being withdrawn. Investigations into a woman's suitability to receive benefits transferred to the Ministry of Pensions in 1918, which saw it as their responsibility to act as a moral compass in the husband's absence. Their stance maintained that the allowance was provided in lieu of the separation of husband and wife and, therefore, if the wife acted in such a way that might cause her husband to successfully seek a divorce then the benefits should no longer be made available. At least forty thousand investigations were conducted by the Ministry and its predecessor, the Statutory Committee, between 1916 and 1920. This equated to one to two percent of qualifying households. Of these, thirteen thousand were upheld and benefits were stopped accordingly.

The programme generally known as the separation allowance, having previously been supported by charities, had strong moral foundations and regular inspections took place to also assess factors such as the cleanliness of the home and children as well as the general standard of the wife's domestic abilities. The idea that there should be a partnership between government and charities was still very apparent in 1934 when Elizabeth Macadam wrote of the 'new philanthropy', in which she called for closer cooperation between the state and voluntary organisations. She did not mean a partnership of equals, but rather voluntary organisations influencing and supplementing public services. In this formulation, voluntary organisations would no longer aim to be the first line of defence for social services as had been the case at the turn of the century.

As demonstrated by the highly moral stance taken in the assessment of the women applying for allowances during World War I, the influence of charities was a positive one in many ways as at least it created the provision of allowances. However, it often came with the imposition of the views of the charity concerned, which may have been more biased and unwelcome than those of an elected government. In this case the theoretically dispassionate government felt it necessary to impose their own morals on the household. In the post WWI era the Ministry of Pensions saw their position as protecting the rights of the husbands in their investigations and subsequent interventions. As the role of the charity diminished, emphasis on the rights of the soldier became the dominant factor.

There was very little meaningful opposition to these policies and practices. A lone voice that of Nina Boyle on behalf of the Women's Freedom League, who spoke out in 1917 asking why all the focus was on the 'moral behaviour' of the woman and none on the men. It was common knowledge that soldiers away from home were themselves rarely faithful and yet they were not held to the same moral account.

Unfortunately, the perspectives of the day did not place equal importance on the fidelity of both partners. The wife's side of the equation was fidelity or chastity while the husband's was a financial duty of care, and as long as that duty of care was maintained then there were no questions asked about his sexual philandering.

Of course it is possible that the lack of dissenting voices was in part caused by a lack of understanding of the programme itself. In her book, *Gender, Welfare, and Citizenship in Britain during the Great War*, Susan Pedersen posits that:

> "Ironically, the shift toward a gender-based model of welfare provision was also unwittingly aided by the responses of feminists and Labour women, who misunderstood the administrative logic underlying the allowance system but welcomed its practical effects. Their confusion was understandable, since the beneficial consequences of the direct payment of support to women and children were far more visible than the Ministry of Pension's attempt to mediate receipt by the husband's consent."

For those in favour of the independence such benefits brought to a woman, there were hopes that it would cause them to speak out in favour of a new status for women going forward. One such woman was Eleanor Rathbone, an Independent MP who was perhaps closer to her Labour women MP colleagues than those from any other party. Eleanor Rathbone wrote that the difference which the separation allowance system has made to many, the sense of security, of ease, of dignity that these women are experiencing for the first time in their lives, is one of the very few good things that the ill-wind of war has created. She further speculated that it would be interesting to see how the women would take it when the war was over and they were asked to go back to their old status of dependency. Being a feminist, Miss Rathbone also hoped that the seeds of 'divine discontent' would have been implanted too deeply in the women to be eradicated.

However, the separation allowance was not intended to provide such independence and was only delivered directly to the wife because there was no means by which to deliver it to the husband. The view that the allowance had created an element of independence and dignity for the recipients was not appreciated by the Ministry of

Pensions and the lobbyists were not strong enough to convince them of the value of continuing with this approach. Once the First World War ended, different provisions were made available that were based on the likelihood of returning soldiers to find work and adequate income. Unemployment benefits and other similar allowances were clearly directed back towards the husband and the only benefit given directly to any wives was a widow's pension.

The related topic of housekeeping and the rights of ownership became key during the early 1940s, and it was one that Edith Summerskill chose to champion. The catalyst was a decision reached by the Oxford County Court between a divorcing couple over who had the rights to housekeeping monies saved over time by the wife. In the case, Blackwell vs. Blackwell, the judge found in favour of the husband, which meant that the £103 kept in a savings account by the wife had to be repaid. The ruling was immediately appealed by Mrs Blackwell's lawyers and, prior to the appeal being heard. Edith Summerskill seized on this case as an opportunity to raise the profile of the issue through the House of Commons and the Attorney General's office. Providing the Attorney General with advance notice of a Parliamentary question, the Lord Chancellor, Sir Claud Schuster, was advised thus:

"Dr Summerskill has the following question on the paper to-day: 'To ask Mr Attorney General whether his attention has been drawn to the decision given in the Oxford County Court to the effect that money which a wife has saved from housekeeping can be claimed by her husband; and whether he will take steps to amend a law which denies a working wife's rights to a share of the family income.'

In essence, the arguments of the day fell into two camps. The lawyers (all of them male) publicly stated that no blanket response could be offered as each case would be different. It would depend upon explicit or implicit agreements between the husband and wife, as well as the circumstances under which the funds were saved. In other words, was the wife depriving the husband or children of anything in order to establish separate means for herself? Dr Summerskill's viewpoint, corroborated by several women's pressure groups, was that a woman was working to create a supportive home for her husband and children and therefore could be said to have earned the money. It also meant that the wife would have demonstrated excellent home economic skills if she had been able to create such a home environment and still put a little something to one side as savings.

The Attorney General's recorded response was carefully guarded:

"I have only seen a newspaper reference to this case. The conclusion seems to depend largely on the nature of the arrangements made between the wage-earner and his wife. I am afraid that it is not possible to undertake in existing circumstances the complicated task of altering the law on this subject." [21]

Although it is not clear of his exact role in this matter, a gentleman by the name of GP Coldstream was, based on the tone, nature and frequency of correspondence in this matter, clearly influential. Unfortunately, his views on women - and women politicians in particular - are clearly expressed in his letters. For example:

> "It occurs to me that it might be wise to tell Dr Summerskill that the case which has stirred her bosom so deeply is at present under appeal, and it is no good putting down any more questions about it for the moment."

Fortunately Dr Summerskill continued her campaign and chose to pursue a slightly different route. It concerned a further question in the House, this time focused on how the Inland Revenue treated savings in an account held by a wife. During her life, the monies were deemed to belong to the husband, but after her death they were seen to be part of her estate for the purposes of calculating death duties. Dr Summerskill proposed that this anomaly should be addressed. Once again the Attorney General side-stepped the issue by claiming he needed case specifics and not generalisations.

Soon after, the Six Point Group, a feminist campaign organisation, weighed into the debate. Their group's stated purposed was to fight for changes in the law in six key areas (hence the name). These were:

1. Satisfactory legislation on child assault;

2. Satisfactory legislation for the widowed mother;

3. Satisfactory legislation for the unmarried mother and her child;

4. Equal rights of guardianship for married parents;

5. Equal pay for teachers;

6. Equal opportunities for men and women in the civil service.

These were the key points established when the group was created in 1921 by Lady Rhondda, and they later evolved into six rather more general points for women's equality: political, occupational, moral, social, economic and legal.

The Six Point Group came forward in 1943 with a proposal to add a significant statement to the 1882 Married Women's Property Act:

> "Provided that the wife may in consideration of services which she may be shown to have rendered to her husband in the home, claim as recompense an equal share with her husband in the family income. Thus the court shall if such an application is made by a wife, cause to be estimated the total of the joint incomes of the husband and wife and the value of their several or joint properties. From this total shall be deducted the estimated average expenses of the joint home and if the sum which the wife has invested in her name does not exceed one half of the surplus income, after the foregoing calculations have

been made, such investments shall not be deemed to be fraudulently made and shall not be transferred and paid to the husband."

As their stated aims were for equality, the statement was very carefully constructed to reflect income generated by both husband and wife. What it does not clearly state is whether 'housekeeping' formed part of the wife's income. If it did then the statement would address the gap in the legislation; if not then the Blackwell vs. Blackwell case would likely have concluded with exactly the same result. Unfortunately merely implying something does not make for a strong argument in court.

So in July 1943 another women's pressure group, the Married Women's Association - who termed themselves the Housewive's Trade Union - posed a further question. This time the focus was on the government-promoted National Savings Movement. Their argument was that the canvassers, going door-to-door and talking almost exclusively to the woman of the house, were encouraging these women to invest by exchanging money for national savings certificates. There were no statistics to indicate what proportion of such money would have been drawn from housekeeping, but the expectation was that it would have been high:

"Nothing in the National Savings Movement's publicity, whether by leaflet or poster or press or radio advertising, has ever made it clear to these housewives that they are accumulating savings to which they have no legal right. The housewife is, in fact, encouraged to believe that the money is hers as she is permitted to purchase savings certificates in her own name with it. The ruling in the Blackwell case seems to point to the fact that both husband and wife are being misled - as also are your canvassers, who are, no doubt, acting in good faith. In light of this ruling, many housewives now have a powerful incentive to spend every penny of the housekeeping money, if not on household necessities, then on themselves."

Despite both of these applications for consideration, the Lord Chancellor was no more open to considering a change to the law, stating on 2 November 1943:

"It appears to me that in suggesting amendments of the Married Women's Property Acts, the feminists are barking up the wrong tree. Substantially, what they want is that a wife should be given some right to the husband's earnings, and apparently irrespective of any bargain, arrangement or contract which is made between the parties...The question whether the radical change in the law desired by Dr Summerskill should be effected is one of general policy upon which I do not feel inclined to express an opinion."

Unfortunately the Lord Chancellor's position was underlined when the Blackwell case was unsuccessfully appealed. Edith Summerskill did not give up, she persevered with Parliamentary questions and went on to sponsor a delegation from the Married Women's Association who wished to meet with the Lord Chancellor.

The meeting was granted for 18th November 1943, and the minutes show that Dr Summerskill and the deputation wished the law amended so that the housewife should have an equal share of the combined incomes of husband and wife after the expense of the house had been met. Dr Summerskill said that the housewife's work was the only work of its kind which carried no right of remuneration and even if she saved out of the housekeeping money the surplus belonged to the husband. Following Dr Summerskill's statement, the representations boiled down to:

1. A proposal that the surplus income when household expenses have been met should be joint property.

2. The inadequacy in some cases of the sum paid to the wife for the running of the household and the expense she is expected to meet out of it.

3. That where a sum is made over to the wife for household expenses or generally to keep things going, savings out of this which are invested should be regarded as joint property.

4. That the wife should have a right to share in furniture purchased out of her husband's earnings, and vice-versa.

Sadly, but not perhaps surprisingly, these points were minimised by the Lord Chancellor. Each was claimed to be either too complex legally, already covered by other legislation, or too insignificant to consider. So while the delegation had the opportunity to lay out their case before the Lord Chancellor, sadly it had no lasting impact and did not result in any alteration in his position.

Edith Summerskill continued her campaign by posing further questions in the House, writing letters to The Times and meeting with different Women's Groups. Although there is no acknowledgement that her efforts had any impact, a letter from the Rt Hon Ernest Bevin to the Rt Hon Sir Donald Summervell on 29th December, 1943 demonstrated a slight softening of the establishment's view:

"The more I come to think about it, the more I become convinced that we should not attempt to deal with this matter unless we are forced to do so. If, however, action is required a presumption that savings of this kind should be joint property would be the neatest way out of an awkward position."

Shortly thereafter, a letter from GP Coldstream backed up this position. In his letter he called attention to an article published in the Law Journal which supported the idea of a common household purse which should be shared equitably between spouses. A further letter, again published in the Law Journal (26th February 1944), further supported this position and it appeared that the tide was finally turning to recognise the value brought to a family by the wife.

Unfortunately the campaign then lost momentum as World War II reached its climax and as the country moved on to the post-war era the Government's attention was redirected accordingly. It is unfortunate that a positive, clear conclusion on this issue was not reached at the time. Although the Married Person's Property Act was updated in 1991, arguably the issue of housekeeping is still alive today given the existence of the wages for housework campaign.

The period 1918 to 1945 was not only a time of huge social upheaval, it was also a time of radical change in the way society governed itself, the way it behaved towards those who carried out manual work, and in how it was beginning to look after those who were poor and needy. Attitudes to women were also changing, though it was often a case of one step forward and two steps back. It was also a time of political idealism. Many Labour Party members were utopian in their outlook, and the phrase "change the world" did not have the clichéd air it does today.

From the perspective of the age, much had been achieved. It was therefore possible that much more could be done. Universal education now existed, medicine was advancing and there was a growing view that it should be accessible to all. The idea of financial support for the poor was taking root following the introduction of the old age pension by Lloyd George in 1908, while the 1942 Beveridge Report paved the way for the modern system of welfare benefits. A family allowance was on the agenda and good quality social housing was becoming a reality.

The early Labour women MPs were very much at the heart of these massive and profound developments. Although most of the time they felt it necessary to take a quietly considered approach, there is little doubt that they were on the side of both working-class people and women and families. The MPs were, of course, encouraged and lobbied by women members of the Labour Party. The vote had been won and women were beginning to realize they could change their lives for the better.

References:

1. Rowntree surveys from 1899 and 1936

2. Gregg and Wadsworth, *The Solidarity Society*, 2001

3. Ellen Wilkinson *Peeps at Politicians*, 1931

4. *The Woman Citizen*, (American Periodical), January 1930

5. Hannah Mitchell, The Hard Way Up, 1967

6. David Jeremiah, *Architecture & Design for the Family in Twentieth Century Britain, 1900-1970*, 2000

7. *The Labour Woman* 1921

8. Municipaldreams. wordpress

9. Hansard 1923

10. Elizabeth Darling and Lesley Whitworth, *Women and the Making of Built Space in England 1870 – 1950*, 2007

11. Ed M J Daunton, *Councillors and Tenants: Local authority housing in English cities 1918-1939*, 1984

12. *Glasgow Rent Strikes*: Red Clydeside Website

13. Deborah Thom, *Nice Girls and Rude Girls: Women Workers in WWI*, 1998

14. *The Socialist Medical Association and the Founding of the NHS*, www.sochealth.co.uk

15. Jane Lewis, The Politics of Motherhood, 1980

16. Pamela Graves, *Labour Women: women in British working class politics 1918 1939*, 1994

17. Margaret Llewelyn Davies, *Life as we have known it by Co-operative Working Women*, 1931

18. Standing Joint Committee on Working Women's Organisations Minutes

19. The Family Allowance System: A Survey of Recent Developments, International Labour Organisation, 1930

20. Susan Pedersen, *Gender, Welfare, and Citizenship in Britain during the Great War*, 1990

21. Hansard 1943.

CHAPTER 4
Peace and Internationalism

Within weeks the horror was fully upon us. That war means the massive, selective slaughter, the killing, maiming, blinding, shell-shocking of men was a fact that no-one could refuse to see.

Mary Agnes Hamilton on the outbreak of World War I in *Remembering Good Friends, 1944*

The impact of the First World War carnage on those women who had lost fathers, husbands, brothers and sons was indeed truly horrifying in both its vastness and its newness. Lives had never been lost on such a huge scale before. It is therefore not surprising that many of those women who had lost loved ones sought out pacifist groups through which they could promote an anti-war agenda. Four of these women, Margaret Bondfield, Mary Agnes Hamilton, Leah Manning and Ellen Wilkinson, were particularly active before and during their time as MPs in the pursuit of peace and international understanding.

As early as 1916, Margaret Bondfield was prepared to place herself in an unpopular position politically to stand up for what she believed in. A vocal opponent of war, she risked being attacked both verbally and physically for speaking out. Other politically-minded women also claimed that Britain's involvement in World War I was the reason for their taking an active role in politics - one of these was Mary Agnes Hamilton. Hamilton and others were likely to have been influenced by Bondfield as is evident from the following quote, taken from the Hamilton's book on Bondfield, which demonstrates how aware she was of Bondfield's perspective on these matters:

> "Practical absorption in the industrial world never made Margaret Bondfield blind or indifferent to its wider connections - least of all the years of the war. She had thought as a socialist while working day in day out for the shop assistants; she thought, more intensely than ever, as an Internationalist in the years of the war and of its bitter aftermath." [1]

In 1916 organised contact between socialist and left-wing women across national boundaries for political purposes was in its infancy. The first account of any kind of international gathering of this kind can be traced back to 1908 when the annual conference of the Women's Labour League received a report of a one day conference for women held during the previous year in Stuttgart prior to the International and Trade Union Conference. Delegates to the Stuttgart conference were very encouraged by meeting comrades from other countries with similar objectives. It was, of course, the fight for the vote which became their main aim.

Regular contacts were established between the International Secretariat and the Women's Labour League (WLL). A second international conference was held in Copenhagen in August 1910, again with the fight for the franchise as its dominant theme. The main outcome of the conference was the introduction of an annual women's day to further the campaign for the vote. Consequently, the first International Socialist Women's Day was held on 19th March 1911 in the Flower Hall in Vienna with the slogan "Equal rights for men and women". International contact between the pioneers of the women's movement had indeed become a reality. Although the First World War inevitably broke the direct ties between socialist women, the Women's International Council was able to receive and print a message from the "Working Women of Great Britain to sisters of other nations." [2] One of the signatories was Marion Phillips, later to become Labour Party Chief Woman Officer and an MP.

Following the First World War international relations, and more specifically securing and maintaining peace, became a high priority at the first major international women's event after the end of the First World War. Held in 1919 in Washington, DC, this conference was an organised, formal affair providing the nascent international women's movement with new gravitas and dignity.

On the policy side, the Standing Joint Committee of International Women's Organisations published a list of the issues women wanted to debate in *The Labour Woman*. These included an end to sweated labour in all countries; hours of work and night work; health conditions in factories and workshops; child labour laws; industrial disease; employment of women in certain trades; and, interestingly, the employment of immigration and coloured labour. Labour women were extremely pleased when it was announced that government advisers to this conference, held under the framework of the League of Nations, should include at least one woman in their number. The newly-formed League of Nations had been enlightened enough to understand that labour legislation involved women as well as men and that women should therefore be represented. Rather than having an agenda that focused specifically on issues concerning the end of the war, the conference instead looked forward and encouraged the working together of different nations in addressing commonly shared post-war challenges. The full agenda was:

1. The eight hour day or forty-eight hour week

2. Problems of unemployment

3. Women's unemployment

4. Employment of children

5. Extension of prohibition of night work for women and an end to the use of white phosphorous in the manufacture of matches

Margaret Bondfield and Mary Macarthur were both selected to attend the conference, and although they were not granted full delegate status they were eligible to vote on the issues as part of the debates. They attended as advisors on those topics of particular relevance to women and while it could be argued that all topics were relevant, there were three of particular concern to Labour women and future Labour Minister Margaret Bondfield, namely women's unemployment, the employment of children and the prohibition of night work for women.

Dr Marion Phillips, member of the Standing Joint Committee of Working Women's Organisations was unable to attend in person. However she and other members (such as Susan Lawrence) were able to contribute through the creation of a leaflet: *Labour Women and International Legislation*. In the leaflet, Dr Phillips concentrated on issues related to the employment of children and Susan Lawrence on unemployment factors. The leaflet was so successful in Washington that it also featured at a subsequent conference in the USA held by the National Women's Trade Union League of America.

The Washington conference reached the following conclusions: that the hours of work should be limited to forty-eight hours per week and eight hours per day with clear overtime restrictions; all-night work for women should be banned; the use of white phosphorous should be discontinued; and the minimum working age for children should be fourteen. Supplementing these conclusions, the Women's Conference in Washington voted for a slightly shorter working week (forty-four hours) and recommended promoting paid maternity leave for all women starting six weeks before the due date.

A follow-up women's conference was held in October 1921 at which Margaret Bondfield, Susan Lawrence and Marion Phillips were the British delegates. The agenda recognised the growing focus for women on matters of peace, and included multi-lateral disarmament, as well as the continuing challenges posed by unemployment.

British women continued to feature heavily on the international stage. Labour women MPs Dr Ethel Bentham, Susan Lawrence and Dr Marion Phillips all attended the International Conference of Labour and Socialist Women in Hamburg on 20th May 1923. Unusually, the main conclusion of this conference was that it should never be held again. Instead efforts should be made to gain a strong female representation on the executive of the mainstream Bureau of the LSI (Labour and Socialist International). However, the British delegates did not concur with this conclusion, believing that an annual international conference was important.

The long time activist Katharine Glasier urged British representatives to press for an annual international conference of women delegates. Opinions changed and a conference was held in Marseilles in August of 1925. In attendance were Marion Phillips, Margaret Bondfield and Dorothy Jewson, amongst others. Following this conference, a new 'International Advisory Committee of Women' met annually to advise the LSI on specific local issues relating to women in different countries. From the British perspective this conference was deemed successful. Particularly noteworthy as far as the Labour Party was concerned was the co-operation between the International Department of the Labour Party and Marion Phillips, the Party's Chief Woman Officer.

The Executive Committee of the International Advisory Committee of Women (IACW) comprised Britain, Germany, Austria and Belgium, and the British contingent included three women: Susan Lawrence, Dorothy Jewson and Agnes Dollan, a former anti-war protester and leading campaigner for improved child health and welfare. The IACW's first conference was held in Brussels in 1928 and featured two significant topics: health and welfare and the deployment of women during times of war. Susan Lawrence contributed to a successfully adopted resolution concerning greater maternity support for women before, during and after birth. This included maternity payments and the provision of domestic support.

The IACW held one more conference in Vienna, in 1931 where the theme was women in the economic system. Again Britain had a strong delegation, including the soon to be elected MP Jennie Adamson who spoke on the role of domestic workers in the home. Sadly the Second World War brought an end to the IACW as political ties were severed, although it is reported that cross-border friendships continued.

Vienna once again became a key meeting place after World War II when the first post-war conference was held in June 1948. Informal international groups had struggled to form during the war; the best known of those for women was the Labour International Socialist Group. This came together when the wife of the Labour Party Secretary invited women refugees to a tea party. Many of these women had attended IACW conferences and they valued the opportunity to continue debates and focus on the challenges the world would face at the conclusion of the war.

The first British women to attend the League of Nations as full delegates were appointed by Ramsay MacDonald in 1929. Established after the First World War, the League of Nations was the first international organisation whose principal mission was to maintain world peace. Its primary goals included preventing wars through collective security and disarmament and settling international disputes through negotiation and arbitration. Nothing if not ambitious, the League also saw itself having a social role and its concerns included labour conditions, just treatment of native inhabitants, the arms trade, global health, prisoners of war and the protection of minorities in Europe.

Mary Agnes Hamilton was one of two women MacDonald sent to the League, the other being Mrs H M Swanick, a well-regarded suffragist and pacifist. Hamilton was viewed as a particular success at the conference and was later quoted as saying:

Mary Agnes Hamilton, 1931

"Geneva in 1929 and 1930 was a genuine International clearinghouse of ideas…There was hard work, and there was goodwill." [3]

Prior to becoming an MP, Mary Agnes (Molly) Hamilton joined the Independent Labour Party (ILP) in 1914 and was an original member of the UDC (Union of Democratic Control), an organisation formed to oppose the close alignment of the military with the government. They opposed conscription and wartime restrictions on civil liberties such as censorship. It was largely funded by the Quakers; as Molly's mother's family had been Quakers there was a shared affinity. By the time she joined the UDC Hamilton was already a published author of both novels and non-fiction. She was also a journalist, writing for *The Economist* from 1913. This was a career she would regularly return to, including being a pioneering woman broadcaster, presenting *The Week in Westminster* for the BBC, originally pitched as an education programme designed to introduce politics and political topics to a female audience. This programme is still broadcast today, but with a broad-ranging perspective that is certainly not restricted only to women.

Despite standing in 1923, Hamilton was not returned to the House of Commons as a Labour MP until 1929 when she won the Blackburn seat and recorded the highest number of votes of any female Labour candidate that year. Hamilton was particularly remembered for her red shoes, an affectation that she felt offered her the female equivalent of the male MP's red tie, and was most definitely not seen by her as a fashion statement. Hamilton fell victim to the disastrous election of 1931 and did not return to Westminster except in her capacity as journalist and biographer. As well as two autobiographies, Hamilton was responsible for biographies of Ramsay MacDonald, Margaret Bonfield, Mary MacArthur and Sidney and Beatrice Webb, together with Abraham Lincoln, Mary Queen of Scots and more. A genuinely prolific writer, Hamilton's journalistic and international experience was rewarded in 1933 when she was made a Governor of the BBC and again in 1940 when she joined the Civil Service and became the head of the United States section of the Ministry of Information.

The First World War only reinforced Molly Hamilton's strong pacifist convictions. However, in common with many others who espoused pacifism in the light of the First World War, her convictions did shift as the world drew closer to the Second World War. The atrocities perpetrated by fascists in Ethiopia and in Spain drove Hamilton to believe that peace at any price was not the way forward. Instead she advocated action against governments anywhere in the world that violated human rights. [4]

In one of her two autobiographies, Hamilton claimed that 1935's League of Nations Union Peace Ballot was a turning point where "persons who ought to know better still often talk as though it had resulted in a demonstration of absolute pacifism. Nothing could be further from the facts." Specifically on Germany and fascism, Hamilton struggled to believe how the majority of the British nation could fail to see the threat Hitler posed:

> "Hitler's screaming voice could not penetrate the sand in which our heads were stuck; instead of reading '*Mein Kampf*' which even in its shockingly bowdlerised English edition was sufficiently alarming, people chatted about 'moral re-armament'."

Before Hitler became well established in Germany and a full-scale war broke out in Europe, the Spanish Civil War erupted and claimed the attention of many in the British Labour and trade union movement. Labour women MPs Leah Manning, Ellen Wilkinson and Edith Summerskill were all directly involved in the efforts to bring democracy back to Spain.

1930s Spain was a country divided. On the left were the Republicans representing the trade unions, the socialists and the working classes. On the right were the Nationalists who represented the military, the affluent landowners and upper classes as well as the Catholic Church. The economic depression experienced worldwide in the early 1930s was clearly one of the catalysts for the civil war as significant unemployment caused general unrest. As an exporter of luxury items such as wine and olive oil, the depression significantly hit Spain's ability to sell its produce across Europe, and other industries, such as iron and steel production, were woefully insufficient to compensate for the deficit. The Republican Government elected in April 1931 was unable to address these issues with the speed, confidence and success needed to quell fears happily fed by the Nationalists. Also feeding the fire of unrest was the demand by two key regions for independence, Catalonia in the North East and the Basque region in the North, both of which had contiguous borders with France. The influence of the Catholic Church was considerable at this time and it was impossible to ignore the antagonism between the Church and the Republican Government. In a highly unpopular move, the Government ceased payment to the priests from the public purse; salaries instead had to be paid from the Church's considerable coffers.

As well as antagonising the Church, the Republican Government felt the only way to balance a failing economy was to enact a number of cost-cutting policies, including reducing the size of the military forcing many senior officers to retire, as well as nationalising major estates across Spain and imposing wage increases on recalcitrant industries. One of the first significant backlashes came from a small segment of the military, but their attempt to overthrow the Republican Government failed in January 1932. However, the seeds of rebellion were sown and continued to grow in the guise of the CEDA (Confederacion Espana de Derechas Autonomas or the Spanish Confederation of Autonomous Right-wing Groups). A highly religious group, this Christian right organisation claimed the Government was pursuing and imposing Marxist politics and needed to be stopped. Its leader, Gil Robles, made several trips to Germany to learn from Nazi rallies how to engage the masses, using these lessons to try and win power by encouraging supporters to act.

Working with like-minded groups, CEDA formed a national election committee to target the major cities of Spain with millions of leaflets and posters and regular showings of campaign films projected on screens in the streets. CEDA gained seats in the 1933 general election in Spain, mainly as a result of a scandal for which the Republican government had to take responsibility. Anza, the Republican leader, was forced to resign after the death of twenty-five people at the hands of the government-backed military while they were attempting to capture known anarchists near Cadiz. This incident was inevitably a severe blow to the Republicans.

CEDA's campaign for power understood the value of targeting the women's vote. The 1933 election was the first in which women in Spain could vote and CEDA took full advantage of opportunities to influence that vote by employing emotional blackmail and its scare tactics in equal measure. These included statements that communism would be the inevitable result of the policies of the Republican Party:

> "…[communism] will tear your children from your arms, your parish church will be destroyed, the husband you love will flee from your side authorised by the divorce law, anarchy will come to the countryside, hunger and misery to your home" [5]

Despite not winning enough votes to form a majority Government, CEDA chose to align itself with the successful centrist Radical Republican Party which resulted in it gaining three ministerial posts. Now with a role in Government, CEDA wasted no time in reversing the policies of the previous government, including removing the limited independence afforded the Catalans. The overthrow of the Asturias miners'

Refugees from Franco

strike by future Spanish dictator General Franco in late 1934 was, perhaps, the first significant step towards civil war. Actions taken on the right as a result of the Asturias incident prompted organised reactions on the left, including the formation of the Popular Front which won a surprise electoral victory in the 1936 general election, perhaps helped by the public reaction to the military intervention in Catalonia. Anticipating such setbacks, the right had already set plans in motion for such an eventuality. General Franco took the lead on a military strategy that resulted in the three year Spanish Civil War. Ultimately a dictatorship was established in Spain under Franco which would last until 1975.

General Franco instigated the civil war with a military coup in Spanish Morocco in July 1936. Franco and his Nationalist forces received support from Italy's National Fascist Party and the Nazis in Germany. Hitler sent air support and armoured ground units to Spain, seeing it as an opportunity for the Nazis to test equipment and tactics in live-fire situations. While Hitler was not yet ready to make his move in Europe, he recognised the value of preliminary action in Western Europe with Italy's support. Hitler did, in fact, encourage Mussolini to supplement the Spanish Nationalist war effort with significant numbers of Italian troops.

The Republicans did, of course, receive outside help, but not to the level of the Nationalists. A small contingent of troops was sent by Russia, but France, Britain and others put their efforts into establishing an embargo on sending troops or arms into Spain. Interestingly, Germany also signed - but ignored - the embargo. The estimated support provided by Germany alone to General Franco equated to £43 million, and within the first year of the Civil War there were an estimated seven thousand German troops supporting the Nationalist military and around sixteen thousand in total throughout the war.

General agreement that Germany was flouting the terms of the previously concluded non-intervention agreement did not lead the signature countries to take any action either in favour of supporting the Spanish Republicans or chastising Germany for its actions. This was common knowledge and prompted many protest speeches in the House of Commons asking why Britain could allow such a flagrant breach of the agreement that resulted in the suffering of so many in Spain.

By the end of 1936 Franco had already seized control of half of the country, including the strategically significant border with Portugal. The Basques and Catalans, already well organised and coordinated regions, put up a more successful defence and were able to withstand Franco's initial advance. This prompted a significant effort by Franco's forces to split the north of Spain from the rest of the country - the Battle of Guadalajara involved around thirty-five thousand soldiers, the majority of whom were Italian. The strategy involved seizing Madrid, Spain's capital, and both sides suffered significant losses - Nationalist casualties were so significant that Franco turned his attention instead to the north of Spain and Bilbao, gradually wearing down Republican resistance with a slow but pressured advance.

By early 1939 an estimated two hundred and fifty thousand soldiers and another two hundred and fifty thousand Republicans had sought refuge across the border in France. Having taken control of Barcelona in the February, Franco again turned to Madrid in March 1939 and successfully took control of the capital just three weeks later.

Britain and France acknowledged the inevitability of Franco's claim on the Spanish leadership in February 1939, before he had taken control of Madrid. The significance of this act was reported around the world including in a small newspaper, *The Advocate*, published in Tasmania. The article, printed on 1st March 1939 said:

"Britain and France to-day announced that they had decided to recognise General Franco's Government in Spain…A communique issued in Paris stated: The Council of Ministers unanimously decided to grant de jure recognition of General Franco. It congratulated M. Berard (the French negotiator) on the happy conclusion of his mission.

Mr Chamberlain said: "The Government has given very serious consideration to the position in Spain and to the action it should take in the light of all the information at its disposal. As a result of the fall of Barcelona and the over-running of Catalonia, General Franco is now in control of the greater part of the Spanish territory both on and beyond the mainland.""

The number of people who died as a result of the Spanish Civil War is unknown. The Nationalists claimed it was one million, but later estimates place the number closer to five hundred thousand. Countless others were subsequently persecuted by the Franco regime over very many years.

The Spanish Civil War was regularly debated in the House of Commons with significant challenge offered by many of the women Labour MPs who wanted to provide help for the Republicans as the democratically elected government. This support took the form of aid as well as challenging Britain's position of non-intervention. One of these women, Leah Manning, took her actions beyond debate. As an extension of her work for education in Britain, she was determined to support those children trapped in the dangerous north of Spain.

Never one to turn away from possible danger, Leah visited Germany almost every year from 1919, though she was forced to stop in 1933 when Hitler rose to power. These experiences likely fed Leah's ardent opposition to fascism. Manning became the Joint-Secretary of the Coordinating Committee Against War and Fascism, as well as working for the Committee for the Relief of the Victims of Fascism. Like Molly Hamilton, Leah Manning's exposure to the fascist movement challenged her previously held pacifist viewpoint. While she retained a general view that it was right to strive for peace, she no longer set military action aside. In fact, the speech which helped return Leah to the House of Commons for Epping made it very clear where she stood following World War II:

> "…we must take our place in a strong world securing organisation which
> will actively protect the peace of the world, by mediation and arbitration
> if possible, but also by having at its disposal an international armed force
> which will make the prohibition of war effective…Above all, remembering
> that 'peace is indivisible', we must allow no misunderstanding to corrupt our
> friendships with our two great allies, the USA and USSR." [6]

To understand Manning's journey from pacifism to selectively supporting military intervention, it is interesting to read her maiden speech in the House of Commons in March 1931 which offered a passionate plea for peace through arbitration, not war:

> "I want to emphasise what is to me…the very simple issue with which
> we are faced… That is the issue as to whether in the future we shall end our
> disputes by war, or whether we shall submit them to arbitration. There has not
> been a war since the dawn of history which could not have been settled by
> arbitration had there been such an instrument as this General Act as part of that
> international machinery. Wars in the past into which this great nation and other
> nations have been plunged by the ruling classes, by Emperors and Kings, by
> great industrialists and capitalists and by the military caste, could have been
> settled, had such an instrument existed, without bloodshed and warfare." [7]

Leah Manning goes to Spain in support of the Republicans

It was Manning's experiences in war-torn Spain that fuelled the change in viewpoint and her subsequent passion to "root out the last remnants of fascism of Europe." In 1934 and the years leading up to the Civil War in Spain, Leah saw the results of the Asturias Miners Strike, an action quashed by Franco's troops. Three thousand miners were killed and thirty to forty thousand imprisoned. Many thousands of others lost their livelihoods.

Despite an official non-interventionist policy, Leah continued to speak out in favour of offering support to the Republicans and lobbied the House of Commons and Clement Attlee to try to engage their sympathies. Alvarez del Vayo, the Minister of Foreign Affairs in the Spanish Popular Front Government, asked Leah to speak out in London on their behalf and tell the government what is happening in Spain. They needed someone who would explain the situation to MPs and ask them to send the Republicans medical supplies and arms.

"It's what we want: someone we know and can trust, who will get
back to England and tell the Government what is happening here…Explain
the situation to all your old friends in Parliament. Get them to send out a
delegation; tell them we must have transport, medical supplies, arms."

In July 1936 Manning became Honorary Secretary of the Spanish Medical Aid Committee. She worked to raise money to pay for medical supplies and staff for deployment in Spain. Manning herself took personal risks when she travelled to

Leah Manning centre and Ellen Wilkinson left

Bilbao in 1937 to support the evacuation of children to Britain by sea. Two days after the fall of Guernica (22nd April 1937) Leah landed in Spain and set about preparing for the mass evacuation:

Despite facing significant resistance in offering help to these refugees, the SS Habana left Bilbao on 21st May 1937. On board were over three thousand eight hundred children, accompanied by fifteen priests, one hundred and twenty young women helpers and ninety-five women teachers.

This was not Manning's only journey to Spain during the Civil War. She returned in July 1938 to visit the hospitals and see where the medical aid was being put to use. After the war Manning continued to maintain ties with Spain and in 1947 she returned to visit a teacher who had been sentenced to death (her sentence was later reduced to ten years in prison). Leah reported feeling that she was under constant surveillance and that Franco's Government was monitoring her visit. In 2002 Leah Manning's efforts to support the Spanish people during the Civil War was recognised with the renaming of a square in Bilbao as *Plaza de Mrs Leah Manning,* and a commemorative plaque was presented to the House of Commons by the Basque Children of '37 Association.

Another of the leading Labour women MPs who took a particular stand against fascism, despite having started from a position of pacifism, was Ellen Wilkinson. During the First World War, Wilkinson supported the *No Conscription Fellowship*, a pacifist organisation that supported those who refused to be conscripted. She was also a member of the Women's International League for Peace and Freedom at this time. This organisation still exists today having broadened its aim to take on board general anti-war campaigning.

Wilkinson co-authored a book with Edward Conze called *Why Fascism?; a Fearless, Provocative Study*. Published in 1934, the book covered three areas: the development of fascism in Europe, specifically Italy and Germany; fascism in practice and in comparison with capitalism and socialism; and finally, the potential for fascism to take a hold in Britain.

Consistent with her contemporaries, Wilkinson regularly spoke out in the House of Commons on the plight of the people of Spain. As an example, on 30th November 1936, Ellen started with a question to Anthony Eden, then Secretary of State for Foreign Affairs, asking what he and the Government intended to do about those who wished to evacuate Spain. Eden's response addressed everyone except the Spanish themselves and so Wilkinson challenged him on this:

> "In view of the present situation, does the right hon. Gentleman not think that the time has arrived to evacuate all the Spaniards and leave the other countries to fight it out?" [8]

No response to this question was recorded and instead the debate moved on to agreements being discussed between Germany, Italy and Japan. Just six months later Ellen, a sponsor and founder member of the Peace Pledge Union (PPU), wrote to resign her position from that organisation despite only having been associated with it for a very short time. She wrote that in view of the Spanish situation 100% pacifism was impossible and that she was sorry to have failed. However she believed that the Peace Pledge Union were right in their goals.

The PPU came into being in 1936 as a result of growing anxiety that there might be another world war. Following a letter from Dick Sheppard to the Manchester Guardian in 1934 a mass meeting was held in the Royal Albert Hall, which led to the PPU's formation. Reflecting the very real concerns at the time, the organisation grew quickly and reached thousands by the outbreak of the Second World War. The organisation's ultimate goal was the elimination of war. Its aims were laid out in a document entitled: *What are you going to do about it? Aims and basis of the Peace Pledge Union* [9] and identified a utopian ideal where the way of life resulted in no need for war:

> "The aim of this and any other peace-movement must then be:
>
> 1. To plan how men may so live that their anxiety and frustration shall not make them violent.

2. To see that this new pattern of living yields them, as well as peace of mind, economic security and a co-operative relationship with their fellow man.

3. To show men how to train themselves so that they can meet with re-assuring goodwill those who are excited and distraught. Those fully trained in this technique can demonstrate that arms are unnecessary in any dealings anywhere with human beings."

In 1936 Ellen joined Clement Attlee on a trip to Spain to provide support to the Republican Party in their increasingly bloody fight against General Franco's insurgence. In response to what she had seen, Wilkinson actively supported the creation of the Dependants Aid Committee in May 1937 to raise money for the families of those men who joined the International Brigade, groups of volunteers from outside of Spain who travelled to join the Republicans in their right to democratic rule.

During World War II Ellen Wilkinson was given responsibility for air raid shelters in Churchill's war-time coalition Government and was instrumental in the introduction of the Morrison shelter. These were steel constructions that could be kept inside the home and even adapted to be part of the furniture such as a table. They could sleep two to three people and were accessed through wire mesh at the side which could be raised and lowered for entry and exit. By this point Ellen Wilkinson had fully reversed her opinion on pacifism.

The other woman politician who regularly appears in recorded House of Commons debates on topics such as fascism was the Independent MP Eleanor Rathbone. Despite holding strong socialist views on issues such as health and welfare and equality of the sexes, Rathbone refused to become a member of the Labour Party.

Rathbone took an early interest in international affairs and India in particular. After reading an article on the subjugation of Indian women and children, she rallied women in Britain through speeches and by authoring a book *Child Marriage: an Indian Minotaur* in 1934. Rathbone ran up against opposition in her efforts to improve the lot of women and children in India and from a place she least expected: progressive and politically active Indian women had been offended by the article which they felt was a racist attack on the social norms in India. It was not until 1935 when the Government of India Act was passed that she was able to make any real progress. She focused on increasing the numbers of women legislators in the new regime. Throughout this time she maintained regular communication with the old-school feminists to ensure she brought them into the Government in ways they may not have been able to achieve on their own.

Other examples of Rathbone's efforts on behalf of British colonies include a December 1929 speech on the horrific act of clitoridectomy in some African countries and the apparent slavery of the vast majority of the women in those countries. This speech, also supported by the Duchess of Atholl, resulted in a cross-party committee being established to focus on the welfare of women in the colonies.

Rathbone's anti-fascist activity started in 1933 when she argued against a policy of conciliation for countries facing Nazi domination. In 1934 she campaigned against Italy's influence over Ethiopia and in 1937 Rathbone - again working with the Duchess of Atholl - met influential politicians in Eastern Europe to talk about the dangers of German intervention in their respective countries. As with many others, it was the action in Spain that Rathbone spoke out against most fervently. She struggled to understand why Britain, a vocal advocate for democracy, was unwilling to stand against the fascist invasion. By the second half of the 1930s, over half of Rathbone's parliamentary questions related to the issue of Spain. As well as speaking out, she took an active role in committees such as a joint committee for Spanish relief. Ellen Wilkinson was also on this committee.

Visiting Spain a number of times from 1937 to 1939, Rathbone's main aim was to gain an understanding of the difficulties faced by refugees. Unfortunately, despite her dogged determination, she was unable to change the opinion of the Foreign Office and had to content herself with small but significant acts of aid to those wanting to flee Spain due to likely persecution under Franco. The time spent on refugees made her an expert and a focus for those wishing to enter Britain. As a result Rathbone established a Parliamentary Committee to assess such requests. Late in 1938 she tried to secure entry for Czech and German socialists and Jews threatened by Nazi occupation, while January 1939 found her in Prague, trying to ensure that such refugees were not simply - in compliance with Nazi wishes - shipped back to Germany. This was indeed a strenuous life for a woman who was almost seventy. While not a Labour Party representative, Eleanor Rathbone's commitment and tenacity does demonstrate the physically and mentally punishing work undertaken by the early women MPs.

Throughout World War II, Rathbone continued to campaign for refugees, even when it placed her in direct opposition to the war-time government. This included establishing The National Committee for the Rescue from Nazi Terror. This Committee lobbied Government on behalf of those at most risk from Nazi invasion and a wide range of proposals - from underground work, to pressure on neutrals and the satellite states, and an actual offer to Hitler to take in all the Jews from occupied lands - made their way from her committee to the Foreign and Home Offices.

Despite this continued effort, Rathbone's efforts were typically ignored or wrapped up in endless bureaucracy. True to form and refusing to be beaten, Rathbone continued her campaign right up to her sudden death from a stroke in 1946. Tributes were sent from humanitarians and politicians from all over the world and a home for refugee children named Eleanor Rathbone was established in Israel, a place with which she felt a great affinity.

Within the world of politics fascinating and sometimes unexpected issues arise. One such topic was the nationality of women who married non-Britons. A letter in the LSE Women's Library archives dated 30th January 1930 recognises the work women MPs such as Ellen Wilkinson were doing to reverse the inequalities surrounding this issue. The letter was sent by Mrs Oliver Strachey, a feminist and Independent politician (she unsuccessfully stood in the 1918, 1922 and 1923 general elections) to a Mrs L Buse (unknown, but based on the contents of the letter likely based outside the UK) on the subject of women's nationality:

"The present position is that although the majority of the House of Commons are sympathetic to the change, and although members like Miss Wilkinson are actively pressing for it, both the last Government and this one have refused to act until they can get agreement first of all with the Dominions and secondly with other European countries."

The letter goes on to talk about an upcoming conference on international law at the Hague and the hopes that, as a woman delegate would be attending, the laws regarding a woman's nationality upon marriage would be addressed:

"The only thing which is at all likely to happen, however, is that married women will regain the right to choose their own nationality. I do not think there is the slightest possibility that any machinery will be set up for helping the Englishwomen married to foreigners trace their husbands if these leave England and return to their own countries. If, however, we do secure the right for women to regain or retain their own nationality that will at any rate be something to the good."

Despite such optimism on the decision to allow women to retain their British nationality on marriage to other nationals, the debates were still raging in the 1940s when the end of the Second World War made this issue particularly pertinent. British women who fell in love with German prisoners of war, and wanted to return with them to Germany once the war was over, had to do so as non-British citizens. At the end of World War II there were over four hundred thousand German prisoners of war still held in Britain, and while there is no official record of how many camps there were they are known to be numbered in the many hundreds. [10] The prisoners were often employed doing manual labour on farms, building sites and roads so, while fraternisation was forbidden and was punishable with imprisonment, there was inevitably a certain amount of exposure. Naturally British women were not allowed to marry German men during the war, but the ban was quickly lifted on cessation of hostilities. In some locations the German prisoners of war were able to mix fairly freely with the local men and women. Naturally therefore, in these times of heightened emotion, relationships were started, love blossomed and proposals of marriage were made. Around twenty-four thousand German men [11] were allowed to stay in the UK after the war, the rest were repatriated to German, the last of whom left in December 1948. The German ban on marrying non-Germans was not lifted until August 1946. [12]

Marriage itself was not the main focus of the debate for the Labour women MPs and Leah Manning in particular. It was instead the citizenship consequences of such decisions. For British men who chose to marry German women there was no change in the man's nationality, regardless of where they subsequently chose to live. Sadly the same rule did not apply to women. Leah Manning took this issue up with her usual enthusiasm, making her case to the House of Commons:

> "As the law stands, the woman, if British, would lose her nationality on marriage to a German [prisoner of war]. No provision could be made for her to live with her husband who, as a prisoner of war, would have to remain in a camp or a hostel under military control; and there could be no relaxation in his favour of restrictions applicable to other prisoners of war. Moreover, no undertaking could be given that the husband would be allowed to remain in this country when he would in ordinary course be due for repatriation. If, therefore, a prisoner of war makes it known that he wishes to marry a woman who is resident here, steps will be taken to see that the considerations which I have mentioned are understood by both parties, and if, nevertheless, they determine to marry, no obstacle will be placed in their way." [13]

There had been fifty four formal applications made to the War Office from British women wishing to marry German prisoners of war by June 1947. Leah Manning took part in a House of Commons debate on the issue she represented a constituent who wished to marry a German prisoner of war. In researching this topic a woman came forward following an advertisement placed in 'The New Statesman' to share a story she remembered from this time which appears to coincide with Leah's involvement in this debate. The story involved a girl in Leah's constituency who had become involved with a PoW at a nearby camp. The girl was remembered as being a little naive and as a result perhaps not fully aware of the consequences of continuing the relationship. When the situation was brought to Leah's attention she immediately challenged the double-standard that would mean this girl could lose her British citizenship. In response to Mr Oliver's earlier statement, Leah asked:

> "Can my Hon. Friend tell me whether my constituent must now make application to the Department to marry this man, or whether some step is to be taken through the War Office for the German prisoner to get into touch with her?"

Unfortunately as this was deemed a new area of debate, the answers were not yet forthcoming:

Mr Oliver Under-Secretary of state for the Home Department replied: "The precise procedure at the present moment I cannot possibly state. Having regard to the statement which has been made, I have no doubt that the lady in question will take the earliest possible and the proper steps to find out the right mode of procedure."

Not surprisingly the issue was very quickly passed on to another department.

Many of the early Labour women MPs were interested in life outside of the UK. Each had her own different reasons for looking further afield. For instance, most of Leah Manning's family moved to the United States when she was just fourteen, so she naturally had the opportunity to visit there fairly often. Leah also had a particular affinity with the Soviet Union, so much so that at times the Labour establishment raised concerns that she may have been converted to Communism. After the Second World War, Leah Manning returned to the Soviet Union for a tour of Russian schools. Her political opponents took full advantage of this and generated significant amounts of negative press concerning her allegiances. She was in fact in Russia on an official visit when the Spanish Civil War broke out in 1936.

Mary Agnes Hamilton also had strong links with the United States. As a political journalist she embarked on several lecture tours and made many friends and connections throughout the country.

Having been born and raised in Australia before coming to Britain, Marion Phillips maintained an international perspective and always sought opportunities to add to the wider international debate. As with almost all of her work, Phillips's contribution to the *Labour Women and International Legislation* leaflet was very well regarded.

Margaret Bondfield was involved in many international activities including a trip to Russia in 1920 where she represented the Trades Union Congress. She had an interest in post-war life in Germany, made official visits to America, and served on various committees and groups such as the International Congress of Working Women and the Women's Peace Crusade. In 1919, having been selected towards the end of the First World War as a delegate to the Congress of the French Federation General du Travail and the American Federation of Labor, Margaret was denied a passport by the British government seemingly on the grounds that women should not travel on their own. One was eventually granted, but it was pointed out to Margaret Bondfield that usually only women on more "correct" positions were allowed to brave the seas.

In her role as Parliamentary Secretary to the Ministry of Labour, Margaret Bondfield took a particular interest in the Commonwealth and emigration (or resettlement) of children in Canada. As a representative of the Overseas Settlement Committee she led a six week delegation to Canada at the end of 1924. The visit was to discuss the continuing placement of around one thousand two hundred children every year from organisations in Britain such as the Salvation Army and

Dr Barnardo's. It also facilitated the investigation of alleged poor treatment of boys on farms [14]. The Bondfield Report, presented to Parliament in December 1924, made the following recommendations:

- the migration of children over the school leaving age should be encouraged;

- that some of the receiving homes should be amalgamated;

- that receiving homes should be inspected prior to placing the child. The delegation concluded that boarding out children in Canadian families brought them little advantage, as such children tended to be exploited by the adopting families.

The numbers of children who emigrated to Canada dramatically decreased over the next five years to the point where, by 1931, only six girls and less than five hundred boys were sent. Interestingly the Great Depression caused several children previously sent to Canada to be returned to the UK as the Canadian economy was no longer in a position to support them.

Bondfield wrote a further report in 1925 called: *The Settlement and Development of the British Commonwealth*. This was published in three sections in *The Labour Magazine*. The first article focused on dispelling the myth that British citizens were only sent overseas to alleviate the unemployment pressures.

> "We have, at the moment, one and a half millions of people who cannot be absorbed into employment under present industrial conditions. It is clear that we have population to spare. The oversea [sic] Dominions, however, want more population. In this country we have 482 person to the square mile; in Canada there are 2.4; in Australia, 1.8; and in New Zealand, 12.2 persons to the square mile."

The second article discussed on the role of women in overseas settlements and an emphasis on family resettlement rather than just individual adults or children:

> "… the importance of the wife was brought home to me on many occasions by the successful settler's remarks that he had his wife to thank for the progress he had made."

Equally, if a particular wife was unable to adapt to her new surroundings, this was deemed significant in the failure of a family's successful integration.

The third article looked at the resettlement of children and teenagers. By the time this article was written, emigration of children to Canada had been happening for fifty years and had resulted in the resettlement of almost one hundred thousand children. The article particularly looked at welfare and potential opportunities for the future for juveniles including the chance to move their families out to join them at a later date.

Overall, the full report, while not sugar-coating the issues, was a piece of positive propaganda for the Overseas Settlement Committee. It sought to encourage support for the various schemes to, in the words of the report itself:

"…[keep] the blood in the body of the Commonwealth, so to speak, in a healthy state of circulation and not allowing it to clot in one part or to become as thin as water in another."

Ellen Wilkinson had also never been narrowly preoccupied with domestic policy. In 1932 she visited India as part of a delegation from the India League. This bore fruit when speaking in a parliamentary debate on India on 18th April 1940 and she felt able to refer to many Indians, including Nehru, as her friends. In the course of her contribution Ellen pleaded against using authoritarian methods against the Indian nationalists, stating that such treatment would project a bad image of Britain to the United States, which at the time was still considering whether to take part in the Second World War.

Ellen's main overseas concern during the 1930s lay closer to home. With her usual intelligence and prescience, Ellen Wilkinson was urging British feminists to resist the discrimination the Nazis in Germany were bringing to bear on women taking paid employment outside the home. Ellen always opposed fascism in every way she possibly could, from helping refugees to passionately opposing non-intervention in Spain. Above all Ellen opposed appeasement, making her passionate views very clear in the House of Commons during one of the most heated debates prior to the outbreak of the Second World War on 24 August 1939. Ellen's forthright words included:

"I cannot enter into the general atmosphere of forgive and forget as regards this present Prime Minister…If the Prime Minister would forgive me for saying so, I think the nation would be much more united if he were not Prime Minister. When he came into office he made it his business to torpedo the system of collective security and refuse to pay the premiums that collective security under the League of Nations meant…Time after time we have had the Prime Minister doing – what? I say putting the narrow interests of his class yes, of his class, the rich, before the national interests." [15]

Such a scathing and even 'unparliamentary' speech was inevitably divisive. Even some of her sympathisers found it distasteful, yet it was one of the most impressive parliamentary speeches on foreign policy made so far by any woman MP. Ellen had, in fact, visited Germany in 1932 where she made a speech to the German Social Democratic Party (SPD) using strikingly Marxist language:

"Amid closed factories and the desolation of world-wide unemployment the sinister, vengeful forces of the fascist counter-revolution talking peace, but intending war, preaching freedom, but conspiring to oppress, promising social justice, but plotting class-domination – have rallied for the supreme onslaught."

Ellen, in common with many on the left, understood the threat posed by fascism. She, of course, spoke out, but tragically for the world her rhetoric and that of her peaceful colleagues was not enough to stop the evil might of Adolf Hitler.

Given the two World Wars 1914 – 1918 and 1939 – 1945, it truly is remarkable that not only socialist women in the UK, but socialist and working-class women across Europe and the British Empire sought to maintain regular, organised contact with each other during these extremely troubled times. Though it was the struggle for the franchise which initially brought them together, a valuable network of international organisations and contacts grew from this tentative beginning. Thankfully the first green shoots were not quashed by the upheaval of the First World War.

Once returned to the House of Commons, many of the Labour women MPs played a full role in international dialogue, genuinely seeking ways to maintain the peace to which they were all deeply committed. Fascism and the rise of Hitler made world peace an unattainable dream from the mid 1930s onwards. Nevertheless, the socialist women kept their international structures intact, to be revived after the Second World War.

References:

1. Ed Lucy Middleton, *Women In The Labour Movement*, 1977, Mary Walker, ch 4, *Labour Women and Internationalism*

2. Women In The Labour Movement, ibid

3. T Zane Reeves, Shoes Along the Danube: Based on a True Story, 2011

4. Ed Peter Brock and Thomas B. Socknat, Challenge to Mars: Essays on Pacifism from 1918 to 1945, 1999

5. Graceta Regional, November, 1933

6. Leah Manning, What I Saw In Spain, 1935

7. Hansard 1931

8. Hansard 1931

9. http://www.peacepalacelibrary.nl/pmfiles/P26-42-004.

10. http://www.theguardian.com/news/datablog/2010/nov/08/prisoner-of-war-camps-uk#data

11. http://www.bbc.co.uk/history/british/britain_wwtwo/german_pows_01.shtml

12. http://specialcollections.vassar.edu/findingaids/bondfield_margaret.html

13. Hansard 1947

14. Hawera & Normanby Star, 16 August 1924

15. Hansard 1939

CHAPTER 5
Education

"A married woman teacher! Such a phenomenon was unheard of in 1914, but I was as pleased as surprised. I had hated the idea of giving up my work"

Leah Manning A Life in Education 1970

Although an MP for just a few brief months in 1931, Leah Manning was to return to the House of Commons in the 1945 Labour landslide to continue her invaluable work representing the Essex constituency of Epping. Despite only occupying a very short time as a Labour woman MP during the inter-war years, Leah Manning deserves credit for her immense and outstanding experience prior to entering Parliament, as well as her effective contribution as an MP during 1931.

Labour Cabinet Minister Barbara Castle has described Leah Manning as "one of the most dynamic Labour women at a critical period in the Party's history" [1]. Always on the left of the Labour Party, Leah was a strong yet sympathetic personality. 'A bit of a character' is a phrase which describes her well. The fact that Leah was only an MP for a few months in 1931 demonstrates yet again just how precarious it was to be a Labour woman MP between the wars.

Education was Leah's life, so much so that she called her autobiography, published in 1970 when she has reached the ripe old age of eighty-four, *A Life in Education*. Teaching was, in fact, one of the few professions open to women when Leah began her training as a teacher in 1906. Fortunately for the young Leah, whose full name was Elizabeth Leah (nee Perrett), education became much more than a job. It was her vocation both before and after her election as an MP.

Born on 14th April 1886 in Burrish Street, Droitwich, Worcestershire, Leah was the oldest of twelve children, though tragically only six survived to maturity. Her parents, Charles William Perrett and Harriet Margaret Tappin, were both officers in the Salvation Army. Harriet had, in fact, been a teacher prior to her marriage, while Charles worked for a time in the family timber business. Since Leah's parents came from opposite sides of the country – her father hailed from Bristol while her mother was a Londoner - it would appear that they had been brought together by their common religion.

Though geographically distant, there were similarities in the family backgrounds of both Leah's parents. Charles's father Thomas Laurence Perrett was a grocer and confectioner while her mother's father George was a timber merchant. What would now be known as evangelical Christianity was a force in the lives of both sets of grandparents. Leah's father's eldest sister, Leah Selina Perrett, was active in the Salvation Army, marrying an Adjutant in the organisation, while Susan Tappin on her mother's side was a member of the Primitive Methodists at their first London Chapel in Coopers Gardens, Shoreditch.

In her early childhood Leah Manning attended St John's School in Bridgewater, Somerset. However, her life in this rural town was not destined to continue, as her parents decided to emigrate to Canada to undertake work for the Salvation Army in the 1890s. Leah did not accompany them, going to live instead with her maternal grandfather, George Tappin and his second wife in Stoke Newington. Separation from their parents at a relatively young age was a harsh fate by modern standards and was shared by both Leah Manning and Margaret Bondfield. Leah's separation, however, did not appear to be as brutal as that of Margaret Bondfield, who was sent away from her family to work in a different part of the country. There is no doubt Leah's grandfather, George Tappin, greatly loved his granddaughter, doting on the teenage girl and looking after her with the utmost care and attention. Maybe because of their close relationship, it is clear George transmitted many of the beliefs he shared with his first wife, Emma Susannah, to Leah, helping to shape the views and values she maintained for the rest of her life.

Leah was sent to school at the Misses Thorns' Select Academy for Young Ladies. In spite of being sceptical about the education provided at this establishment, the young Leah found inspiration from the Reverend Stewart Headlam, a controversial and lively man who first came into contact with Leah following a performance in a school play. A member of the London School Board, Headlam became an important figure in Leah's life, a mentor and a friend. His views and his faith had a profound and lasting influence on the young woman she was becoming. Headlam opposed church schools, campaigned for the repeal of the Blasphemy Act, supported the public house, the theatre, the ballet and the music hall and also urged the nationalisation of land. Encouraging her in her studies, Headlam donated books to the young Leah and found her a teaching position in a boys' school. To the horror of her puritanical grandparents, Headlam introduced Leah to the theatre, which became a lifelong passion. Headlam, in fact, stood bail for Oscar Wilde whose harsh treatment was also condemned by her grandparents. Leah began to attend services at St Margaret's Church, Westminster where Headlam preached. Some 40 years later as an MP she would be a member of its Parliamentary Church Council. Her Christian Socialism dating from these early formative years remained with her right to the end.

On reaching the appropriate age, Leah hoped to go to university. Stewart Headlam suggested she attend Homerton Teacher Training College in Cambridge. Leah applied and was given a place, thereby starting the next important phase in her life. Leah Manning was about to find her true vocation. Arriving in Cambridge in 1906, the young Leah revelled in her new found freedom.

"I won't pretend I was a very serious student. I worked hard at the subjects that interested me, especially those that concerned my training as a teacher and utterly neglected others. This gave me time for the social life at college which I enjoyed enormously." [2]

As a student from 1906 – 1908 Leah swam, played tennis and hockey, made friends and generally enjoyed college life. She became chairman of the debating society and drama club, secretary of the Student Christian Union and, importantly, took the initiative in forming the Socialist League. Leah's involvement in the Socialist League undoubtedly developed her ever expanding interest in politics. During these student days Leah met Hugh Dalton, the future Labour Chancellor of the Exchequer, who became a lifelong friend. After being introduced by Dalton, Leah joined the University Fabian Society and the Cambridge Independent Labour Party. She was one of the first, but by no means the last, of the many politicians who gained their spurs in student politics.

On completing her course with an 'A' teaching mark, Leah was at the front of the queue for the sought after London teaching posts, yet after some consideration she opted to stay in Cambridge and teach at New Street:

"…the practice school regarded with horror by every student, where the children were so poor, so undernourished, and so apathetic, that it seemed impossible to stroke one spark of interest from them." [3]

Founded 1846 to provide non-denominational education to the children of Barnwell, New Street School was a sorry example of the inadequacies of the education system at the time. Education for children whose parents could not afford school fees consisted of free elementary schools up to the age of fourteen. The New School soon became known as the "Ragged School", located as it was in a very deprived and neglected part of Cambridge. By 1901 there were one hundred and one children on the roll. Leah found working at the school a hard chore and she had to cope with between seventy and eighty children in a class. Leah recalls in her autobiography:

"Poor mites! Under-fed, over-worked, lacking sleep, I often wished for a bit of real naughtiness, but they didn't have enough spirit,"

Going on to say:

"When I look at the splendid, robust youngsters of today [1970], with children's allowances, school milk and school meals, and the whole paraphernalia of the Welfare State protecting them, it seems incredible that little more than half a century ago, girls and boys should have been so destitute." [4]

In response to this appalling state of affairs, Leah began to campaign for free milk for the poorest. She discovered to her horror that before the education service's Medical Officer could advise milk he must certify that the child was already suffering malnutrition. The cruelty and inadequacy was brought into sharp relief when Leah witnessed the death of a student from what was effectively starvation. Having summoned the press to a meeting of the local Trades and Labour Council, Leah delivered an impassioned plea for action:

> "So because of permissive legislation your Education Committee must wait until a child is in its coffin, dead of malnutrition, before the Medical Officer can certify that it is in need of milk." [5]

Leah was immediately summoned before the Education Committee and told either to withdraw and apologise for these remarks or leave her job. Leah, with her indomitable spirit, not to mention her tough inner resourcefulness, appealed to the National Union of Teachers and her colleagues on the Cambridge Branch of the National Council of Women, managing in the end to avoid either of these stark alternatives.

Leah's other major contribution to New Street School was the setting up of an after school play centre, modelled on an example from North America which she had come across during a visit to see her parents. The new evening centre, designed to provide support and recreation for the slum children, proved very successful. The venture won Leah acclaim from a wide spectrum of the community.

As might have been expected in those years before the First World War, Leah married before her thirtieth birthday. At the age of twenty-seven, five years after taking up her post at the 'Ragged School', she became Mrs Manning, wife of William Henry Manning, an assistant at the University of Cambridge Solar Physics Laboratory, the son of a Fenland market gardener. A shadowy figure, William Manning was, interestingly, a Liberal in politics, though given the political outlook of her beloved grandfather, Leah probably would not have found this too difficult to accept, at least in the early days of her marriage. Leah and her new husband soon moved to a house at the Solar Physics Laboratory where William lived until 1949, though Leah is not listed at that address after 1934. Leah's relationship with William's mother seems to have been strained at times, at least on the matter of personal appearance. Speaking about her mother-in-law, Leah contrasts her own lack of interest in her appearance to Mrs Manning senior, who was the exact opposite:

> "[My mother-in-law was] a very beautiful woman, tall, graceful and faultlessly made up – which amused me, since I had never (indeed never have) sported so much as a dab of powder on my nose." [6]

We shall probably never know what, if any, strong feelings lay behind these telling words. Meanwhile, Mrs Manning junior had expected to resign her teaching post

Leah Manning VAD 1914

as was customary on marriage. However, at the outbreak of the First World War the Cambridge education authority relaxed the marriage bar, enabling Leah Manning to go on teaching. She therefore continued at the New School and in keeping with the wartime spirit took on other work as well.

In common with many of her socialist colleagues, Leah was opposed to the war. She did, of course, wish to help in a peaceful fashion and therefore volunteered as a VAD (Voluntary Aid Detachment) nurse at the First Eastern General Hospital mobilised on 5th August 1914. Over the next four years the hospital dealt with many thousands of injured servicemen. Leah's philosophy at this time of great turbulence and suffering was typical of her general outlook:

"If I couldn't stop men from being torn to pieces, perhaps I could do something to comfort and assuage." [7]

The VADs had made up their own words to the "Tipperary" tune to keep themselves going:

It's a big, big rush to the cloakroom

It's a big, big rush to go;

It's a big, big crush in the cloakroom,

It's the biggest crush I know.

Goodbye to all neatness,

Farewell, tidy hair;

It's a big, big rush to the cloakroom,

But we all get there. [8]

Leah, already a teacher and a nurse, somehow also found time to become a member of the Insurance Committee at Cambridge and later Secretary of the Borough Food Control Committee. There seems little doubt that even the redoubtable Leah was overdoing it, even more so since pregnancy was added to her personal agenda at the end of 1917. In mid-1918 Leah Manning gave birth to her only child, a daughter who tragically only lived for three weeks. Leah suffered what she called a 'crise de nerfs' during her pregnancy and wrote in her autobiography with commendable honesty:

"In the Summer my baby daughter was born. She only survived three weeks. I couldn't grieve. All my tears were shed." [9]

It seems from this time onwards that Leah and William grew apart. There were no further children and little is said of them spending time in public together.

Following the deep personal loss of her baby, Leah perhaps unsurprisingly, threw herself anew into her political work. By the end of the First World War in 1918 she was Chairman of the Cambridge Trades Council and the Labour Party. Returning from the Labour Party annual conference in November that year, Leah was full of enthusiasm for the forthcoming general election and determined that both of the Cambridge seats should be contested by Labour candidates. In the event, the Labour Party did just that, selecting reverend Rhonnda Williams, a non-conformist minister, together with the longstanding Cambridge County Councillor printing worker Albert Stubbs. The Labour campaign radiated confidence with such eminent speakers as Sidney Webb and Margaret Macmillan.

Though politically challenging, the election was not good for Leah on a personal level. Her Liberal husband, William, worked for the Cambridge Liberal candidate, former Cabinet Minister Rt Hon E S Montague. During the course of the campaign husband and wife had to avoid any chance of personal confrontation, hardly an ideal way of behaving. Leah's personal difficulties were no doubt compounded by what was a disappointing result for Labour. The Conservative won the city seat while E S Montague was the comfortable winner in the county.

Leah returned to the electoral fray to campaign for her friend Hugh Dalton, Labour candidate in a by-election in Cambridge in 1922. Leah was, as ever, completely unconstrained by any assumptions about appropriate behaviour for a married woman:

> "Our out-door meetings were exciting, but sometimes a little rough.
> I remember an occasion when Maurice Dobb ("band-box Bertie") and I
> were addressing a huge crowd from a cart on Market Square. A score of
> undergraduates got between the shafts and ran us around the Square. I couldn't
> keep my balance, and since soon began, indelicately, to show my underwear.
> Maurice pushed me down on a chair and clung desperately to it himself, while
> the men continued their frolic and cries of 'good old ginger' and 'good old
> Bertie'." [10]

Despite the fun and the obvious hard work, Dalton lost by over three thousand votes.

Leah, of course, remained immersed in her own public service. By the time of the 1922 by-election she was a member of the Labour Party Advisory Committee on Education and a magistrate in Cambridge. In addition to Leah, two women had been appointed Justices of the Peace in the city in 1920, in the first list of women justices in the United Kingdom. Leah Manning had, indeed, made history. 1920 proved a propitious year for her since she was also appointed head teacher of the new Vinery Road Open Air School in Cambridge.

Neither of these prestigious positions dampened Leah's radical ardour or inhibited her political activities. During the General Strike from 3rd to 12th May 1926 Leah played a leading part in the Cambridge Council of Action, helping to organise the 'bedders', laundry workers and other female employees. A less successful endeavour involving Leah was the campaign to unionise the Chivers Jam Factory after the management locked in their workers – mainly women – during the midday break.

Needless to say, Leah was a staunch member of her trade union, the National Union of Teachers (NUT). In 1924 she was elected to the Union's Executive Committee becoming Chairman of the NUT Law Committee and a member of the Burnham Committee on teachers' pay. Ever the radical, Leah associated with the "forward" movement in the Union, which was left-wing or Liberal in politics. She worked closely with figures like W G Cove, President of the NUT in 1922 who went on to become a Labour MP, W Hill (President 1928), and Frederick Mander, later General Secretary. In 1930 Leah gained the true recognition she deserved

Leah Manning, National Union of Teachers Jubilee President 1930

by being elected as NUT President at the NUT Diamond Jubilee Conference in Bournemouth. Despite the large proportion of women in teaching at this time, Leah Manning was only the fourth woman to achieve this distinction.

Fortunately for Leah, her period of office as NUT President coincided with the second Labour Government which tried, amongst other things, to raise the school leaving age to fifteen. As President of the NUT, Leah had several discussions with Sir Charles Trevelyan, President of the Board of Education, on this issue. In recognition of her wide-ranging knowledge and experience in education, Trevelyan appointed Leah to one of his Departmental Committees dealing with private schools. Leah was finally getting a taste of politics at national level. She was now ready to seek selection to enter the House of Commons and was nominated on to the NUT Parliamentary List, the first woman to achieve this position.

Despite her long experience in the Labour and trade union movement, Leah's journey to becoming a Member of Parliament was by no means plain sailing. In 1930 and at the age of fifty-four, Leah expected to become the Labour candidate in a by-election in the Bristol East constituency caused by the death of the Labour incumbent Walter Baker. Leah had, in fact, been approved by the Union of Post Office Workers who had sponsored Baker. However, the Labour Party hierarchy had other ideas and parachuted in the young Sir Stafford Cripps, recently made Solicitor-General (despite not being an MP, and following the death of Sir James Melville, the previous holder of the post). True to form Leah Manning would not be treated so dismisively. She was furious that she was being passed over, refusing to give way. She was only persuaded when her old friend Hugh Dalton, now Under Secretary of State at the Foreign Office, forcefully twisted her arm. The second Labour Government was facing serious problems and Leah did not want to seem more concerned about herself than the Party. According to her autobiography Dalton's words to her were serious despite his light-hearted tone:

> "Uncle Arthur [Arthur Henderson, Labour Party Secretary and Treasurer] asks me to tell you [Leah] that he will make this a test of your loyalty to the Party." [11]

Leah eventually gave way with bad grace but never forgave Stafford Cripps.

As may happen in politics, all was not lost. Early in 1931 the Labour woman MP Ethel Bentham, who had represented Islington East since the 1929 general election and shared Leah's interest in under-nourished children, died suddenly. Following his promise to Leah that she would get the next by-election as a reward for her loyalty over Bristol East, Arthur Henderson made sure he delivered. Leah Manning thus became the first woman parliamentary candidate under the NUT banner.

On Thursday 19th February 1931 Leah Manning was elected Member of Parliament for Islington East, beating the Conservative candidate Thelma Cazalet by more than three thousand votes, thanks in large part to the Empire Crusade contender splitting Conservative support. Leah was proud to take her place in the House of Commons with the other Labour women MPs, including Susan Lawrence, Marion Phillips, Margaret Bondfield, Ellen Wilkinson, Lucy Noel-Buxton, Cynthia Mosely and Jennie Lee. Islington East had been a hard fought contest which Labour had not really hoped to win, coming as it did in the midst of the deep economic crisis.

In the House of Commons Leah naturally took a particular interest in education, keeping in close touch with the NUT. She was even approached to take a junior post at the Board of Education, but did not accept the offer. Leah's own teaching experiences in the Cambridge slums reflected the general state of elementary education in most of Britain:

Leah Manning and her Conservative opponent Thelma Cazalet in the East Islington
by-election 1931

"It is not unusual in old-fashioned schools to find cramped surroundings
and no proper playground, no separate hall which is not used as a classroom,
classrooms made to accommodate sixty – one hundred children, and sometimes
one large room in which four or more classes are taught together." [12]

The majority of elementary school classes had well over forty pupils, many
with more than seventy. Given these dire conditions it may come as a surprise to
learn that the First World War had ignited an interest in education largely due to
considerations of national efficiency and a desire for progressive reconstruction.
Women in the Labour Party were well aware that education was a prominent
concern. An article in the *The Labour Woman* publication in 1916 made the point
that:

"The war has brought great changes, and one of these is the need of
recasting the system of education. Unless the working people make up their
minds and say what they want and keep on saying it, the system of education
in this country will go on being imposed on them from the top, will become
more and more commercialized and more and more directed to making a good
industrial employee rather than a fine man or woman of the citizen." [13]

The Education Act introduced by the Liberal Minister H A L Fisher in 1918 raised the school leaving age to fourteen and required local authorities to draw up education plans. Fisher himself made an astute observation about the attitude of Labour MPs towards education, stating:

"My personal appeals to Labour benches went unanswered. Though far-reaching and ambitious resolutions were passed at Labour Conferences …. There was no great show of precipitancy in the House of Commons in supporting a measure for the extension of education…Whether out of modesty or indifference the voice of Labour… was seldom heard." [14]

Fisher's views seem in hindsight to have been a little harsh on the Labour Party. Official Labour Party Committees, women in the Party, and Labour women MPs regularly discussed matters to do with schooling. In *Labour and the New Social Order* published in 1918 the Party set out general goals, calling for a nationalised education system based on the principle of social equality, an approach shaped by the experiences of active Labour Party members who were to a large extent self-taught through private reading and attending evening classes. This "sense of having pulled themselves up by their bootstraps fostered not a rigid egalitarianism, but a strong sense of the unequal chances which were given to the children of poor parents" [15] ensured that Labour Party policy was to provide a distinctive secondary education for adolescence rather than making provision merely by extending elementary education.

The Labour Party Advisory Committee on Education, of which Leah Manning was a member, produced a policy document in 1922. One of its key objectives adopted as Labour Party policy was:

"…both the improvement of primary education and the development of secondary education to such a point that all normal children, irrespective of the income, class or occupation of their parents, may be transferred at the age of eleven from the primary or preparatory school to one type or another of secondary school and remain in the latter to the age of sixteen." [16]

A Fabian Tract written by Barbara Drake and published in the same year as the Labour Party policy document, made other important demands, including the need for more secondary schools:

"For practical reasons it would be idle to suggest that the present shortage of secondary schools should be made good at once. The Advisory Committee of the Labour Party has therefore put forward the very moderate proposal that local authorities should provide places for at least twenty children between eleven and sixteen for every thousand of the general population in their areas." [17]

Drake also emphasised that at least seventy-five per cent of children were capable of benefitting from secondary education.

Susan Lawrence, MP for East Ham, spoke to the Labour Women's Conference in 1924 on education as well as other matters. She attempted to draw attention to additional hindrances to working-class children caused by the prevailing environment and ethos in the grammar schools across England and Wales. Since 1907 all grant-aided secondary schools had been required to provide at least twenty-five per cent of their places as free scholarships for students from elementary schools, and the poorer pupils found it hard to keep up with their middle class peers. As Lawrence said:

> "The standard and expense in games, in clothes, and generally in the social life of the school is too often set by and for the richer children." [18]

Despite her reservations about grammar schools, Susan Lawrence called for a great expansion of advanced education in a pamphlet also produced in 1924. She called for maintenance scholarships and the doubling of the numbers in secondary schools from ten to twenty per thousand of the population, a position not far removed from that adopted by Barbara Drake two years earlier. Lawrence put it succinctly:

> "There are those who now have children of fourteen years or so at the elementary schools, and who are wondering what they are to do with them, who dread for their children the miserable skirmish for underpaid jobs, and who are yet forced by the sheer pressure of poverty to take their children from the safety of the school, on the chance of bringing a little money into the home." [19]

In the same year as Lawrence's pamphlet the Labour President of the Education Board did, in fact, make some very tentative steps towards answering the demands for the expansion of advanced education, specifically allowing local education authorities to introduce bye-laws to raise the school leaving age to fifteen. Trevelyan's softly, softly approach was helped, and may have been partly shaped, by the argument that putting up the age when children could leave school would alleviate unemployment. At the same time he also had to recognise that increasing the national school leaving age was a financial impossibility.

Leah Manning spoke eloquently about what Susan Lawrence had called advanced education during a debate on education funding in the House of Commons in July 1931 shortly after her election as the Member of Islington East and just months before the Labour Prime Minster, Ramsey MacDonald, resigned to form the National Government. Always on the left of the Labour Party, Leah clearly felt she should pursue reform of the education system at the same time the Government was dramatically cutting back on public spending.

Referring to children who have a high intelligence standard, Leah pinpointed the problem that secondary education in England was not free for children over the age of fourteen. She dismissed the arguments that money was scarce, pleading with the minister to fight those enemies of reaction who tell him there is not enough money. In her customary outspoken way Leah demanded:

"What is he [the Minister] there for? He is the champion of education. Other people scramble for money, and why should he not scramble for money? I know what I would do in his place. The Ministry would not stand for more than a few months if I could not get what I wanted. The great thing for which we of this Party stand...is free secondary education."

In the same debate Leah gave sound arguments for free secondary education:

"twenty-nine per cent of fee payers in secondary schools were passing examinations and fifty-four per cent of the free placers were passing examinations. We have had a lot of talk about anomalies lately, but municipal secondary schools in which fees have to be paid are an anomaly in a State system of education. The children who are paying fees are filling places which could be better filled by children with a greater ability to profit by the teaching which is given. Why should fee-paying children be subsidised to the extent of two thirds of the cost of their education when we have boys and girls in the elementary schools waiting on the doorstep to push forward into secondary education?" [20]

Leah continued by raising a point of specific interest in 1931:

"The position is a very grave one this year....With the jump in the birth rate in 1920 there will be hundreds upon hundreds of boys and girls in working-class homes who are eleven years of age this year and who, because our reactionary education authorities will not increase the number of free places, will be disappointed in the scholarship they thought they would get."

While Leah Manning chose to join and later lead the National Union of Teachers (NUT), open to both men and women, another women-only teaching union was in operation during the same period. The National Union of Women Teachers (NUWT), founded as the Equal Pay League within the NUT, was renamed the National Federation of Women Teachers in 1906, its primary aim being to secure pay parity between women and men in the teaching profession. Lack of progress towards this goal led to the establishment of an independent body, the National Union of Women Teachers, in 1920. While the NUWT continued to campaign for equal pay in teaching it also, along with other feminist organisations, fought to extend the franchise to all women on the same terms as men, which was achieved by the 1929 general election. The NUWT also, of course, became involved in a wide variety of professional issues, including cuts in educational budgets in the early 1920s and again in the 1930s, restrictions on the employment of married women, the engagement of unqualified teachers, and the practice of appointing man as head teachers in most cases where girls' and boys' schools were amalgamated.

As an organisation for women teachers, it is not surprising that the NUWT championed the extension of educational opportunities for girls and their access to the professions. They also supported the maintenance of separate infant schools with their own head teachers as opportunities for the advancement of women teachers. The NUWT not only opposed corporal punishment in schools – a radical view at the time – but also supported the introduction of sex education. They also wanted to see educational films made for children.

During the Second World War the NUWT was concerned to secure the continuity of education for children evacuated from the cities. Once the war ended the fight for equal pay was vigorously resumed. The NUWT also favoured raising the school leaving age to fifteen. Once pay parity was achieved in 1955, NUWT membership began to fall, due also perhaps to changing social attitudes towards separate organisations for women and men. The union was eventually wound up in 1961.

It is today an article of faith that education opens doors to the extent that half of our school students progress to higher education. While university hardly appeared at all in the Labour Party's thinking during the inter-war years, it is very striking that of the women elected as Labour MPs during the inter-war years only three did not continue their education beyond elementary school, the most prominent being Margaret Bondfield. Having spent a year as a pupil teacher Margaret, in common with almost all working-class young women, was forced by economic circumstances to earn her own living. The other two who never made it beyond free schooling up to the age of fourteen were Agnes Hardie and Jennie Adamson, both from social backgrounds not dissimilar to that of Bondfield.

There were, however, two working-class women, Ellen Wilkinson and Jennie Lee, who did go to university, an unusual and difficult achievement at the time, especially for young women. Ellen Wilkinson progressed from elementary school to secondary school with the help of additional teaching, gained by attending lectures on theological subjects delivered at her Methodist chapel. Ellen won a pupil teacher bursary which enabled her to attend as a pupil teacher for two and a half days at the pupil teachers' centre in Manchester, while spending the other half of the week teaching in elementary schools. In 1910 Ellen won the Jones Open History Scholarship, open to any UK student, and went to Manchester University.

Jennie Lee's earlier years followed a similar pattern in that she went to the local elementary which was supplemented by her socialist Sunday school. Jennie then moved on to Cowdenbeath's new Higher Grade School which was unusually well-equipped, free and open to all children who passed their elementary leaving examinations. She managed to stay on until the age of fifteen after agreeing to her parents' demands that she take night classes in shorthand, typing and bookkeeping. When Jennie came top of the class they relented and she went to Edinburgh University, having already obtained local authority and Carnegie grants. She trained

Jennie Lee the politician in 1937

as a teacher and also studied law gaining an ordinary MA, her teacher's certificate and an LLB (law degree) in 1926.

Of the Labour women elected to the House of Commons between 1918 and 1939, nine were from what would have been seen at the time as relatively comfortable middle-class backgrounds. Three of them had gained places at Cambridge University. Two of these three were, in fact, from the first Labour women returned to the House of Commons in 1923. Susan Lawrence, the daughter of a prosperous solicitor, went to Newnham College Cambridge after first being taught at home, attending the Francis Holland School in London's Baker Street and then spending time at University College London. Dorothy Jewson, the other Cambridge graduate amongst the first three, was equally privileged, having been educated at Cheltenham Ladies' College before being admitted to Girton College. The third Cambridge graduate was Mary Agnes Hamilton. She attended Aberdeen Girls' High School and Glasgow Girls' High School before going to the University of Kiel for seven months to learn German. Later that year she arrived at Newnham College, as the

Lady Cynthia Mosley MP with her sister at Cap D'Antibes August 1931

Mathilde Blind scholar reading classics for two years, then economics as the major element of the history tripos.

The remaining six middle-class Labour women MPs at this time all had university degrees. Ruth Dalton had a fairly typical education for a young woman from her background at this time, consisting of a combination of private tutoring and formal schooling and going on to study sociology at the London School of Economics. Ethel Bentham, Leah Manning's predecessor in East Islington, was educated at Alexandra School and College, Dublin at a time when the whole of Ireland was still part of the United Kingdom. Ethel went on to train as a doctor at the London School of Medicine for Women at the age of almost thirty, gaining her certificate in medicine in 1893. Interestingly there was another Labour woman doctor in the House during this period, Edith Summerskill, who, after attending Eltham Hill grammar school, began her medical training in 1918. This took place at two London hospitals - King's College and Charing Cross.

In addition to Leah Manning, whose background was probably more middle than working-class, the other two Labour women MPs from a relatively well-off, as opposed to either a working-class or a wealthy family, were Lucy Noel Buxton and Marion Phillips. Noel Buxton went to school at St James' in West Malvern. Phillips is unusual in that she was born outside the United Kingdom, in Australia, having been educated at the Presbyterian Ladies' College in Melbourne from 1897 – 98, and then at Ormond College and Melbourne University studying philosophy and history. Phillips came to England in 1904 to study at the London School of Economics. In 1907 she graduated with a DSc (Econ) with a doctoral thesis on the development of New South Wales which she published under the title of *A Colonial Autocracy*.

Two of the remaining four Labour women MPs during this period were, surprisingly, from even wealthier backgrounds than those best described as middle-class, coming from families which could be described as almost aristocratic. Cynthia Mosely's early education was in India before being sent to boarding school. She then went on to take various courses at the LSE. Edith Picton-Turbevill had an upper-class schooling, a mixture of private tuition and boarding school, after which she trained for a year in mission work at a Mildmay school in London which included 'practical work' in the slums of Shoreditch. Picton-Turbevill then returned to India to take up a post with the Young Womens' Christian Association.

Five of these first Labour women MPs took up teaching professionally, almost certainly because it was seen at the time as an acceptable career choice for women. Three of them - Leah Manning, Dorothy Jewson and Jennie Lee – were elementary school teachers while Marion Phillips spent some time lecturing at the LSE. Ellen Wilkinson had been a teacher prior to attending university. Given that nearly a third of the sixteen Labour women MPs elected during the inter-war years had experience of working in education, it may have been expected that they would show an interest in educational issues once they arrived in Parliament. However, with the exception of Leah Manning this does not appear to have been the case before 1939. Ellen Wilkinson, of course, was appointed Education Minster in the 1945 Labour Government, while Jennie Lee went on to make important contributions in making further and higher education more accessible during her period as a minister in the 1960s, particularly through her efforts to promote the Open University plans.

Though there is little doubt that the dire state of the economy, the Great Depression and massive levels of unemployment drove education off the agenda in the 1930s, there was perhaps another reason for Labour's reluctance to engage fully with the issue; namely that working class people growing up in the early twentieth century had to teach themselves if they were to learn anything at all, a state of affairs alluded to in the 1918 Labour Party policy document *Labour and the New Social Order*. H A L Fisher may well have had a point when he commented in his unfinished autobiography that:

> "Hard bitten old half-timers like Philip Snowden and J R Clynes cherished, I believe, a secret liking for the system under which they had been schooled for success. What had been good enough for them, what had so easily fashioned those qualities of fortitude and independence which had brought them to the front of political battle could not be without value." [21]

Ellen Wilkinson (third from the left in the back row) at Ardwick Higher Grade School

The Snowden/Clynes view seems to have been shared by Ellen Wilkinson. Her father's political creed: "I have pulled myself out of the gutter, why can't they?" certainly appears to have rubbed off on her in that Ellen did have faith in the system as it functioned for her own education.

"Once I started at infant school, I went through the 'broad highway of state education', through elementary school, higher grade school to the university. I won my first scholarship at the age of eleven, and from that time paid for my own education by scholarships till I left the university…From the higher grade school on, the buildings were excellent, and the teaching, I suppose… admirable". [22]

Ellen went on to say that she left school with the conviction that there was nothing I couldn't do:

"I learned all too early in life that a clear decisive voice and a confident manner could get one through ninety per cent of all the difficulties in life." [23]

That Ellen Wilkinson attained her startlingly high level of educational achievement was not at all typical of girls in general in the 1920s and 1930s. Ellen herself was aggrieved that:

"…boy rebels had a better time, although the scheme [elementary schools] was co-educational until fourteen years of age. The master would often give extra time, lend books and so on to a bright lad. I never remember such encouragement. I was only a girl anyway." [23]

Ellen's experience was more than likely typical. Indeed, discrimination against girls was given official sanction in the 1923 Hadow Report *The Differences of the Curriculum for Boys and Girls*. The Hadow Committee was clearly anxious about the pressures on girls due to the relatively heavy domestic duties often performed by them in their homes. Hence the Report recommended that external examinations for girls should be reduced and that girls should take the First School Examination a year later than boys. Furthermore, girls should be protected from "physical fatigue and nervous overstrain", that they should be required to do less homework than boys and that the girls' morning session should not exceed more than three and a half hours.

Just as girls faced widely differing expectations from boys in the 1920s, working-class children of both sexes received nothing like the standard of education offered to those who were better off. In her House of Commons speech in 1931, Leah Manning berated the education system for failing bright working-class children. By the end of the 1930s opportunities for elementary school pupils were severely restricted, with about one in eight reaching secondary school and only one in 170 boys making it to university. In 1937 the New Fabian Research Bureau produced a document setting out a programme for a future socialist government. It is perhaps unfortunate that this new paper showed little evolution in their thinking since the earlier paper produced by Barbara Drake in 1922, despite the fact that Drake herself edited the 1937 effort. It reiterated the desire for an education system in which all children progressed logically through nurseries, primary and secondary schools, supported in some cases by maintenance allowances and free school meals.

Picking up on the concerns voiced by Labour women MPs, articles written in *The Labour Woman*, and the observations of educationalists, the Fabian Research Bureau devoted a section in their programme to the health of the school child. It argued that the school medical service should form an integral part of the public health department saying:

"If the state accepts the duty of educating its future citizens, and if disease can be shown, as it certainly can, to interfere with the efficiency of this education, it is surely the duty of the state to accept full responsibility for the removal of this disability, and allow no financial consideration to interfere with the efficient education of its future citizens" [24].

The paper also discussed school meals, an idea similarly championed by the National Union of Women Teachers. As long ago as 1922 the Standing Joint Committee of Working Women's Organisations (SJC), comprising representatives from the Labour Party and the trade union movement, had proposed a scheme for universal provision as part of a general scheme of family maintenance which had never been pursued by government.

Child welfare is inextricably bound up with education. It was also the basis on which women in the Labour Party campaigned for the nurseries advocated by the Fabian Society. Articles on the subject appeared in *Labour Woman*. Talking about the need for a national campaign for nursery schools, a piece published in January 1928 framed the argument thus:

> "The little toddler is an object of pity these days in the crowded poor hopes of the workers. Mothers are worried to death through unemployment and underemployment of their menfolk. When a new baby arrives it is the little toddler that has to manage and misses the mother's care mostly."

The debate continued on the pages of *The Labour Woman* and in March of the same year another article told the readers in no uncertain terms that:

> "The working women and young girls of England must come in now like a flood and save millions of little ones who have no nursery and no real nurture today."

Although they were appalled by the child poverty they had seen at first hand, the campaign for nurseries does not appear to have been taken up by any of the Labour women MPs at this time. There were no doubt many reasons for this, chief among them the nation's parlous economic state. Another barrier may have been that the women MPs did not wish to challenge the prevailing view that children were the sole responsibility of the mother. Nurseries could be seen as challenging this received wisdom. The Labour women elected to the House of Commons during the 1920s and 1930s may not have felt their positions were strong enough to put forward the controversial proposition that children had fathers as well as mothers, and that society in general should ensure the health, welfare and education of its young charges.

Neither Margaret McMillan, the veteran campaigner for improvement in children's wellbeing, nor the National Union of Women Teachers (NUWT), had such qualms. While the NUWT campaigned for the general establishment of nursery schools, Margaret Macmillan in her work *The Nursery School*, first written in 1919 and republished in 1930, sets out her view that rearing children was not the sole responsibility of the mother:

> "Nurseries and Nursery Schools are wanted simply because little children want nurses. They, being children, need that very important kind of early education called nurture. Can this be given and given entirely by, let us say, the average mother? The well-to-do mother never attempts to do it alone. She engages a nurse, perhaps also a governess...The working-class mother in her tiny home has no help at all." [25]

To further her argument McMillan claimed that her goal of collective action by mothers to be given nurseries was analogous to the way in which working men had secured the privileges of the middle-class such as public libraries. Men had done this by campaigning together and demanding collective provision, so mothers must do the same for what mattered to them. This was radical, not to say feminist, talk in 1930. It is therefore perhaps not surprising the Labour women MPs did not wish to go along with it. McMillan did not stop there. She advocated a long nine hour day for the nurseries:

> "It may be said, and is said often 'This will take the whole burden of parenthood off the mother and the father'. In so far as the mother is concerned it has the opposite effect. New responsibility is acquired through increase in power and knowledge." [26]

McMillan also proposed that each nursery should have a Mothers' Club which would meet weekly to socialise, mend and sew clothes and receive lectures on practical matters, including education and diet as well as social affairs.

Yet McMillan did have sound educational reasons as well for demanding nurseries for working-class children. She believed, perhaps ahead of her time, that they would provide a foundation for more demanding education later in children's lives.

> "The Nursery School, if it is a real place of nurture, and not merely where babies are 'minded' till they are five, will affect our whole education system powerfully and very rapidly. It will quickly raise the possible level of culture and attainment in schools, beginning with the junior schools." [27]

McMillan found a surprising ally in Sir William Henry Hadow whose Report in 1933 on infant and nursery schools commended care for pre-school children:

> "The fundamental purpose of the nursery school is to 'provide an environment in which the health of the young child – physical, mental and moral – can be safeguarded. Its aim is 'not so much to implant knowledge and the habits which civilised adults find useful, as to aid and supplement the natural growth of the normal child.' The Report also maintained that, "The treatment of children in the earliest years of life – including an 'open air environment' – is of the utmost importance if later emotional development is to be satisfactory. Between the ages of two and five children should be 'surrounded with objects and materials which will afford scope for experiment and exploration. The young child should not be expected to perform tasks which require 'fine work with hands and fingers'. The ideas presented to him should be 'very simple and few at a time; oral lessons should be short and closely related to the child's practical interests." [28]

Unfortunately the nurseries which would have made such a difference to the lives of working-class mothers and their children remained a pipe-dream throughout the inter-war years. The demand that poor women receive the help wealthier women were able to buy was a non-starter, despite the massive impact it would have made in improving the health and welfare of the kind of children who came into Leah Manning's care at the 'Ragged School'. Other priorities deemed more essential had yet to be overcome. With no real champions in Parliament, those women in the Labour Party and the country who so desperately needed this kind of support had to wait a very long time for it to arrive.

The same is true, albeit it in a different way, for those who wished to see a more egalitarian approach to secondary education. In 1929 the National Association of Labour Teachers (NALT), formed in 1926 and renamed the Socialist Education Association in 1961, made an argument for 'multilateral' schools. Acting as a pressure group and forum for debate on educational issues in the Labour Party, the NALT held national conferences, regional meetings and produced publications. It was an influential body and was especially strong in London. The 1929 NALT document *Education, A Policy* stated:

"If all types of pupil shared a common school life it would help towards the highly desirable end of eliminating class and social distinction which are bound to persist, if different fixed-types of schools are set up for children of the same age range."

The idea of multilateral schools was, of course, the forerunner to the modern comprehensive system. The NALT argument that schooling should be totally egalitarian was sadly far too utopian for the Labour Party in the 1930s. Perhaps because of this, NALT's proposals for multilateral schools received only scant attention among Labour Party activists, although the TUC did take up the concept in 1934. NALT's position was, however, strengthened to some extent when Labour won the London County Council (LCC) in 1935, though not enough for multilateral education to be taken on board by government.

The fact that the multilateral ideal did not take off was by no means the end of the road for reform of the education system; it was becoming ever clearer that the elementary schools did not deliver for the vast majority of children. Sir William Henry Hadow presided over no less than six reports between 1923 and 1933 dealing with educational organisation. One of Hadow's recommendations – stratification at the age of eleven - was singled out by Leah Manning in her House of Commons speech in 1931:

"I do not believe in the stratification of our children at the age of 11. There are no means of telling at that early and tender age what a child is going to be…" [29]

Hadow had, if fact, recommended in the 1926 Report *Education of the Adolescent* that primary education should end at age eleven with all 'normal' children going on to some form of post primary education. He also recommended that the school leaving age be raised to fifteen, if possible by 1932, and that new forms of leaving examinations be developed. It was, however, the Spens Report *Secondary education with special reference to grammar and technical high schools* published in 1938 that recommended there should be three types of secondary schools – modern schools, technical high schools and grammar schools with children selected at the age of eleven. This provided the template for the future. Interestingly the Spens Report committee did not rule out the adoption of multilateral schools but thought them "too subversive a change." Following Spens, the 1944 Education Act introduced the tripartite system.

As Minister for Education, Ellen Wilkinson opposed the comprehensivisation of schools. Her stance was very likely informed by her own background; personal circumstances seemed to have been much to the fore in the Labour politician's thinking on education at this time. At the 1946 Labour Conference, Ellen Wilkinson told delegates:

> "I was born into a working-class home, and I had to fight my own way through to the University."

Ellen believed in an ideal of meritocracy rather than increased access to education.

While Ellen believed in education organised on a system rewarding merit, it is striking when looking across the range of education policy between the wars that virtually no reference is made to children with disabilities, with the exception of the 1931 Hadow Report which made a number of recommendations relating to the education of "retarded" children. Specifically, the Hadow Report thought that the extent of their retardation should be investigated and responded to appropriately, and that special schools for the severely retarded should be closely related to the general educational system. A further report from Hadow in 1933 emphasises the importance of detecting early signs of retardation and discovering the causes, but does not recommend special schooling for "retarded" children at an early age.

Leah Manning was, as ever, one of the few to talk about "retarded" children, or "mental deficiency" as she called it. Leah was very clear that the best was not being done for mentally defective children. Speaking on the subject at some length in a House of Commons debate Leah pointed out that:

> "…it is a matter of the greatest gravity to this country that the mentally defective child has been completely neglected…I have asked for the number of schools which have been erected for the mentally defective child during the past few years, and have received the reply that in 1926 the number was five; in 1927, four; in 1928, none, and in 1930, one."

Leah went on to explain the position of 'mentally defective' children in some detail:

"…there are 340,000 mental defectives in this country…from 1906 to 1929 mental deficiency doubled…there are fifty-five per cent more mentally defective children in rural areas than in urban areas…the incidence per 1,000 school children in urban areas is 20.7 and in rural areas 39.7."

During her speech Leah Manning stressed that she had conducted a thorough investigation into mental deficiency and that her figures were correct, stating:

"The grave social problem of the sub-cultural mentally defective is to be found in the very poorest homes in this country and not in well-to-do homes… sixty-one per cent come from homes below the average and twenty-five per cent from the poorest slum homes. This is why I say it is a social and not a pathological problem. We find these cases associated with the worst of our social problems – chronic pauperism, habitual crime and illegitimacy…One school for mentally defective children per year is not enough; it is a disgrace."
(30)

Needless to say little concrete action came out of Leah Manning's championing of children with learning difficulties, just as so many other ideas about how education could be better delivered did not come to fruition during the 1920s and 1930s.

The inter-war years were, despite the seeming lack of progress in some areas, a time when social conditions were appraised and often found wanting. Ideas for improvement proved plentiful but many of them fell by the wayside, at least as far as education was concerned. Neither did the Labour women in the House of Commons, with the honourable exception of Leah Manning, appear to make much of a contribution. The times, especially after the 1929 Wall Street crash, were hard, making any kind of social progress more difficult than ever, and this may have been a factor in the Labour women MPs avoiding issues which required increased public spending. There was, of course, more to it than that. Women were not really established in either the House of Commons or the Labour Party. The early Labour women MPs had little choice but to toe the Party line. As far as education was concerned, it was only the fearless Leah Manning who really spoke out in Parliament.

Eventually it was the Conservative President of the Board of Education who introduced educational reform in 1944. The Education Act of that year took on board the proposals set out in the Spens Report and introduced a tri-partite system of grammar, technical and secondary modern schools which provided the basis for the way state education was run in England and Wales for the next twenty years. It is, however, notable that when the Education Bill had its second reading in the House of Commons on 19th January 1944, not one of the Labour women MPs spoke in the debate. Whether this was out of concern for upsetting the war-time coalition consensus, or because they truly believed the three tiers were the best solution, is not clear. All that is recorded is their collective silence.

Having lost her seat in 1931, Leah Manning contested the north-eastern seat of Sunderland in the General Election on 14th November 1935. Not only was the local press hostile to her, supporting the rival National candidate, but Leah was also attacked in a leaflet distributed to a large number of Catholic voters early on the morning of polling day. The leaflet contained passages from the writings of Ethel Mannin, a distinguished novelist at the time who was outspoken on life and sex in a manner, though commonplace now, was unacceptable in the 1930s. An outspoken passage had been extracted away from its context and underneath, referring to Leah Manning, were the words, "do you want a woman who holds such views to represent you in Westminster?" Leah says she knew as soon as she saw the leaflet that the Catholics would desert her and that:

> "I have never been able to decide whether it was a genuine mistake in which the Catholics were not involved, or whether it was a trick engineered by the Tories." [31]

Leah did, in fact, lose in 1935 and went to work at the NUT headquarters in Hamilton House. She returned to the House of Commons in the 1945 Labour landslide.

References:

1. Ron Bill and Stan Newens, *Leah Manning,* 1991

2. Leah Manning, *A Life in Education,* 1970

3. Leah Manning, ibid

4. Leah Manning, ibid

5. Leah Manning, ibid

6. *Leah Manning,* Ron Bill and Stan Newens, 1991

7. First Eastern General Hospital (Cambridge) Gazette 7.12.1915 reprinted in Bill and Newens, ibid

8. Leah Manning, ibid

9. Leah Manning, ibid

10. Leah Manning, ibid

11. Leah Manning, ibid

12. Leah Manning, ibid

13. Barbara Drake, *Some Problems of Education,* Fabian Tract No 198, 1922

14. Rodney Barker*, Education and Politics 1900 – 1951: a study of the Labour Party,* 1972

15. Rodney Barker, ibid

16. Richard Tawney, *Secondary Education for All: A policy for Labour,* Labour Party Advisory Committee on Education, 1922

17. Barbara Drake, ibid

18. Susan Lawrence, *A New Spirit in Education,* Pamphlet, 1924

19. Hansard, ibid

20. Hansard, *1931*

21. Rodney Barker, *ibid*

22. Ed Margot Oxford, *Myself When I Was Young*, 1938

23. Ed Margot Oxford, ibid

24. Barbara Drake ed, *State Education: An Immediate Programme for a Socialist Government,* New Fabian Research Bureau, 1937

25. Margaret McMillan, *The Nursery School,* 1930

26. Margaret McMillan, ibid

27. Margaret McMillan, ibid

28. Derek Gillard, *The Hadow Reports: an introduction,* 2006

29. Hansard *1931*

30. Hansard 1944

31. Leah Manning, ibid

CHAPTER 6

The House of Commons and the Labour Party

"[I am] sick of hearing about the sacred rights of private property. I want to hear about the sacred rights of human life"

Ellen Wilkinson The Town that was Murdered, 1939

Ellen Wilkinson, returned in the General Election of 1924 was, for two years, the only Labour woman on the Opposition benches. She was one of the outstanding characters of her generation, not only as far as the women politicians were concerned but across the entire spectrum of public life. Born in October 1891, 'Red Ellen', so called because of her red hair and her red views, was only 33 when she entered the House of Commons. She was to stay there until 1931, winning her seat of Middlesborough East for a second time in May 1929. In common with all the other Labour women MPs she lost out in the 1931 election and it took until 1935 for her to return to Parliament, this time representing Jarrow, a town with one of the worst unemployment records in England.

Both heavy industrial towns in north-east England, Middlesborough and Jarrow were similar constituencies with seemingly intractable problems to challenge their elected representative. By the time of Ellen's election in 1924 Middlesborough had an unemployment rate of 10,000 within a population of 136,000. Jarrow in 1935 was, if anything, in a worse state, ably and passionately narrated by Ellen herself in her 1939 book *The Town that was Murdered*. To have been selected by the Labour Party in such bastions of male trade union power was an achievement in itself; Ellen went on to succeed in the House of Commons, on behalf of her constituents and the people of Britain as a whole.

Ellen Wilkinson will be forever remembered for her leading role in the 1936 Jarrow Crusade, the hunger march which has passed into folk-lore. Ellen made sure she understood Jarrow's complicated industrial problems with her accustomed attention to detail. Jarrow depended on one industry, shipbuilding, and Palmers shipyard in particular. Since the First World War a third of Britain's shipyards had been closed down due to falling demand, including Palmers in 1934. According to Richie Calder in the *Daily Herald*, Palmers was the only shipbuilding concern

Ellen Wilkinson as a toddler

Ellen Wilkinson at home

to handle the whole process from iron quarrying and steel-making to the launching of ships [1]. Incredibly after Palmers was sold the purchasers were prevented from using the site for shipbuilding for the next forty years.

The whole tragic story of Jarrow is brought into sharp relief by the fact that demand for shipbuilding was increasing by the mid-1930s due to rearmament. The Iron and Steel Federation was formed as a precondition to the establishment of import tariffs and was forced on the Government, effectively preventing the regeneration of steel production in Jarrow. A plan to make Jarrow the centre of a vast new integrated steel plant was distrusted by rival steel makers who believed it would depress their prices and the proposal was effectively sabotaged. Ellen understood what was going on, later spelling it out in *The Town that was Murdered,* murdered in fact by capitalism which brought huge suffering to the people of Jarrow.

Ellen saw the family poverty and misery caused by unemployment, which was to her the true essence of men being out of work. By the time of her election there were skilled craftsmen in Jarrow who had not been in paid work for fifteen years. In December 1932 nearly eighty per cent of the insured population was out of work, and this level remained until the outbreak of war. Living conditions in Jarrow at this time were truly appalling. When the Conservative Health Minister in the National Government, Sir Hilton Young, stated that there was no real starvation or malnutrition in her constituency Ellen challenged him in the House of Commons, quoting the case of three young male workers who had died in quick succession from malnutrition, and whom the local vicar had described as "looking like eggshells" – fine on the outside but when faced with an infection in winter they had cracked [2]. Red Ellen's answer to unemployment and its consequent suffering was sound socialist planning. As it turned out, it was wartime demand which alleviated her constituency's and the country's grave and seemingly insoluble problems.

Women were actively discouraged from taking part in the Jarrow Crusade. However Ellen Wilkinson was determined to support this stand against the continued unemployment. Each member of the march was medically checked and issued with a kitbag before they set off with Ellen leading the way on 5th October 1936. Strictly non-political, the march was organised by Jarrow Town Council, supervised by the Town Clerk and supported by the Mayor. The crusaders were to present an eleven thousand signature petition at the Bar of the House of Commons, which duly took place after they arrived in London on the last day of October. The march had been well organised, maintaining an air of purpose and respectability in order to increase its effectiveness. Ellen herself marched on foot for large portions, if not the whole, of the Crusade.

Ellen was a feisty and forthright woman with an indomitable spirit who inevitably spoke her mind. Shakespeare's words in Midsummer Night's Dream "though she be but little she is fierce" could have been written for Red Ellen. Her appearance, only four feet ten inches tall and slightly built, belied her power and conviction, not to mention her outstanding intelligence, evidenced by her winning the Jones

Open History Scholarship to Manchester University. Vibrant and also, according to some, coquettish, Ellen Wilkinson was a world away from the Edwardian gentlemen's club atmosphere of the House of Commons in the inter-war years. Ellen was popular with the press and the public; her arrival in Parliament was greeted by a huge media frenzy, even more than that accorded to the Conservative Nancy Astor, the first women MP to take her seat in the Commons. Those who knew and supported Ellen were enchanted by her charm and vitality. What is more, according to Susan Lawrence, Ellen had an "instinct for the big thing". [3]

People such as Ellen Wilkinson, especially women, always have their detractors. To some, particularly her political opponents, Ellen was viewed as a self-obsessed 'self-publicist' and emotional to boot. To be a fearless, pugnacious and outspoken woman is to court opprobrium even today. In 1924, the year of young Ellen's election, such a woman was indeed a rarity in the public sphere. What is more, Ellen dared to challenge the prevailing orthodoxy regarding the appropriate dress for women MPs. While the Conservative MP Nancy Astor and the few other women in Parliament wore black, believing that being a woman was different enough without drawing attention to oneself, Ellen decidedly broke the dress convention, turning up to the House of Commons in February 1925 in a vivid green dress.

Ellen also defied convention in more important matters. In her usual fashion she was determined to get stuck in. The constituency Ellen represented in 1924, Middlesborough East, suffered from poverty and unemployment in the same way as Jarrow. Ellen felt the plight of her constituents was too urgent for her to wait the customary seven months before making her maiden speech. On 10th December 1924, the second day of the parliamentary session, Ellen rose to make her mark. Far from the conventional inoffensive maiden speech devoid of political content, and in her self-possessed and assured speaking style, Ellen ranged across the issues dear to her and her Party's heart; the need for increased unemployment benefits, factory law reform and votes for women.

As well as conviction in her message, her voice proved to be a priceless political asset. Twenty-odd years later fellow Labour MP Jack Lawson summed it up:

> "In her voice was power and music with a tone like that of a well-cast bell and she knew how to use it at mighty conferences, open air demonstrations, indoor meetings or in the House …. even though the despatch box was too high for her, and she had to stand aside from it." [4]

Ellen Wilkinson was joined by Margaret Bondfield after her victory in the Wallsend by-election in 1926. Following the 'flapper election' in 1929, not only was Susan Lawrence re-elected to Parliament but the roll-call of Labour women in the House of Commons rose to eleven. In addition to Wilkinson, Bondfield and Lawrence, there was also: Ethel Bentham, Ruth Dalton, Agnes Hamilton, Jennie Lee, Lady Cynthia Mosely, Dr Marion Phillips, Edith Picton-Turbervill, and Lady Noel Buxton who won a by-election in 1930. Labour women in the House of Commons

Labour women in the 1929 Parliament

were still a rare species, comprising a tiny percentage of the two hundred and eighty-seven strong Parliamentary Labour Party. Yet one of their number, Margaret Bondfield, was appointed the first women Cabinet Minister, while Susan Lawrence became Parliamentary Secretary to the Ministry of Health, with Ellen Wilkinson as her Parliamentary Private Secretary. Mary Agnes (Molly) Hamilton would become Parliamentary Private Secretary to the Postmaster General in 1931.

1929 proved to be the high point for returning Labour women MPs during the period 1918 - 1945; Labour's success was not to be repeated until 1945. The fact that every single one of the Labour women MPs lost their seats in 1931 demonstrates just how precarious their position was. During this period, and indeed later, it was rare for women to be selected in safe Labour seats. This, taken together with their lack of numerical strength, helps explain why from the mid-1920s all the Labour women MPs, including Ellen Wilkinson, worked with the Party grain, toeing the Party line. Only Cynthia Mosely, among the first Labour women MPs, broke ranks as a result of the 1931 crisis. Taking six months off from Parliament she spent her time warning the country of the defects of the Labour government. It will hardly come as a surprise to know that such behaviour sounded the death knell for her career in the House of Commons.

Despite the apparent lack of respect of their colleagues, these leading Labour women MPs wanted to collaborate with men to end class exploitation. They would almost certainly have accepted Herbert Morrison's declaration that "I do not think so much about men and women. I think about the human race." The fact that working through the Labour Party ran the risk of upsetting non-party feminists certainly did not concern Bondfield, who felt that those whom she saw as middle-class feminist zealots had no idea about the realities of working-class life.

A number of strong feminist organisations existed in the 1920s and 1930s. Some, such as the National Union of Societies for Equal Citizenship (NUSEC), had been formed before women were granted the franchise and continued to campaign to equality in more general matters after the 1929 general election. The NUSEC in particular sought reform in laws considered discriminatory, such as family law and prostitution. Having changed its name to the National Council for Equal Citizenship, the organisation was wound up at the end of the Second World War. In 1926 the Open Door Council, a breakaway group from the NUSEC, was formed following disagreements with the NUSEC about the social reforms passed by the 1924 Labour Government.

Other significant feminist groups included the Six Point Group, which included the novelist Rebecca West. Essentially a lobbying organisation, the Six Point Group aimed at political, occupational, moral, social, economic and legal equality both in Britain and internationally, taking their cause to the League of Nations. Politically allied with the Open Door Council, the Six Point Group was largely middle-class, as were both the NUSEC and Open Door Council itself.

While expressing caustic views on middle-class feminists, who they thought did not understand what life was like for the majority of women, Bondfield and

Wilkinson, along with the other Labour women MPs elected during the 1920s and 1930s, did, in fact, champion women's interests, especially in matters to do with working conditions. Indeed, on her promotion in 1929, Margaret Bondfield stated in her autobiography *A Life's Work* that she was selected as the first woman cabinet minister not out of any personal virtue, but because all of her life had been spent in the training ground of corporate bodies. She was, she said, the product of the work of hundreds of thousands of unknown names.

The truth was quite simple. As Labour Party representatives, the early Labour women MPs did not see women's concerns as distinct from those of the wider struggle against exploitation. If Ellen Wilkinson had been forced to choose between feminism and socialism, she would have chosen socialism. However, the Labour women MPs at this time thought the democratic overlap between socialism and feminism was so great that the choice never presented itself. In 1928 Ellen spoke up for equal franchise for women and men, while in 1936 she voiced strong support for equal pay. Yet her true loyalties came to the fore in 1944 when she had to choose between equal pay and supporting the wartime coalition. In the three confidence votes on the issue held in the House of Commons, Ellen backed the Government every time.

Whilst it is true to say that once they arrived in Parliament most of the Labour women MPs generally took the view that socialism and women's interests were virtually indistinguishable, it is also the case that almost all of them had been involved in votes for women campaigns, organising women in trade unions (often in separate women's sections) and participating in the Labour Party women's organisation. Given that, in common with the rest of British society during the inter-war years, working class bodies were constituted on the basis of separate spheres for women and men, it was perhaps inevitable that this route was an important training ground for the first Labour women MPs.

However, each of them could choose between the numerous avenues open to women activists in the Labour, trade union and women's suffrage movements. Of the first three Labour MPs returned in 1923, Margaret Bondfield had belonged to the Women's Trade Union League (WTUL) before entering Parliament and, together with Mary Macarthur, founded the National Federation of Women Workers. In 1906 she helped get the Women's Labour League off the ground. Susan Lawrence was also involved in the WTUL while Dorothy Jewson joined the militant Women's Social and Political Union in 1911 when she returned to Norwich after leaving Cambridge. Ellen Wilkinson was also a campaigner for women's votes, taking up an organising position with the National Union of Women's Suffrage Societies in 1913.

Others had similar experiences. Edith Picton-Turbervill was a non-militant suffragist. Another suffragist, Jennie Adamson, became a member of the Labour Party National Women's Advisory Committee, while Marion Phillips was appointed as the Party's Chief Woman Officer in 1918. Two of what could be described as the more middle class of the Labour women MPs, took a rather different approach.

Susan Lawrence campaigning
in the rain

Susan Lawrence demanding
equal votes for women

Labour Women's Conference 1936. Society was still divided into separate sphere for women and men

A professional broadcaster, Mary Agnes Hamilton presented the first ever edition of the radio programme *The Week in Westminster*, designed to teach women about politics. Dr Edith Summerskill took the liberty of calling herself a feminist and was a founder member in 1938 of the Married Women's Association which aimed for more equality between married women and men. The gender divide and the concept of separate spheres was, inevitably, writ large in the House of Commons between 1918 and 1945. The number of women from all parties elected during this period tells its own story:

1918:	1
1922:	2
1923:	8
1924:	4
1929:	14
1931:	15
1935:	9

Number of women elected from all parties between 1918-1935.

Women's representation in the House of Commons was to remain shamefully low for the next half-century. The widespread belief that public life should be reserved for men and family life for women remained remarkably well-entrenched for a long time after the Second World War. The technicalities of getting into Parliament only reflected this view of society, and it was not until the General Election of 1997, when the Labour Party introduced all-women shortlists for its parliamentary selection process, that the number of women began to rise by any significant amount.

During the 1920s and 1930s a woman sometimes found it easier to enter Parliament if it could be claimed that she represented a man, the so-called male equivalence. Two of the Labour women MPs come into this category, Ruth Dalton and Lady Lucy Noel Buxton. Both were elected in by-elections. Ruth Dalton, wife of the future Chancellor of the Exchequer Hugh Dalton, was returned for Bishop Aukland in February 1929, only to leave Parliament at the general election just a few months later to allow her husband to take up the seat. Ruth Dalton holds the joint record, along with Margo MacDonald, for the shortest serving MP. Lady Lucy-Noel Buxton entered the House of Commons in 1930 having won a by-election in North Norfolk following her husband Philip's elevation to the peerage.

Unsurprisingly at a time when most women did not undertake regular paid work outside the home, the inter-war MPs were disproportionately older, unmarried and childless. Margaret Bondfield, Susan Lawrence, Ellen Wilkinson, Ethel Bentham, Mary Agnes Hamilton, Marion Phillips and Edith Picton Turbervill all answered to this description. While these women had passed up the chance of family life, the male dominated House of Commons often made the most of its opportunities to question women's suitability for non-domestic work of any kind. One of the most bizarre examples of such behaviour took place in a debate in 1943 which assumed that the menopause disqualified women between forty-five and fifty for war work, when Dr Russell Thomas talked about the "physiological and anatomical changes" and "the great internal stress" associated with this time in a woman's life.[5]

Once in Parliament, these very few women found it was much easier to attract the Speaker's eye on social questions or education than on what were considered the more weighty matters of state - the economy, foreign affairs or War Office matters. Foreign Secretary Austen Chamberlain (in the two sessions of 1924 – 25 and 1926) and Sir Leslie Hore-Belishar as Secretary of State for War (in the two sessions of 1937 – 38 and 1938 – 39) each contributed a sixth as much to debates in the general area of defence, empire and foreign policy as that contributed by all thirty-eight of the women MPs from all the political parties between 1919 and 1945.

While men and women at this time continued to occupy separate spheres, everyone in Britain was acutely aware of the class divide. According to Professor Brian Harrison, nothing angered the Conservative Nancy Astor more than class-conscious rhetoric. Ellen Wilkinson was the first of the Labour women MPs to

Dr Marion Phillips MP claims to have been the first woman MP to have invented a really convenient House of Commons uniform which she is wearing in this picture. It consists of a well-cut overall of thick crepe-de-chine lined with bright silk and buttons over her dress

make speeches specifically referencing class and as she herself put it to "take up the cudgels". Between 1929 and 1931 Jennie Lee, who was even younger than Ellen Wilkinson when first elected, made intellectually powerful attacks on capitalism. During the late 1930s Agnes Hardie, sister-in-law to Keir Hardie, Labour's early Leader, made speeches which were perhaps even more class conscious than those of either Wilkinson or Lee.

Although Labour women MPs have never managed to transform the House of Commons, the very few elected between 1918 and 1945 did make significant and generally well-regarded contributions to debates in the Chamber. Maybe because they were so few, or perhaps because they needed to prove women could be effective parliamentarians, the women members across the political divide felt a special obligation to speak in debates. Professor Harrison has analysed their performance between 1919 and 1945, telling us that men contributed 30,000,000 lines to Hansard and women 550,035. According to the *Parliamentary Gazette* Susan Lawrence was the sixth most prolific debater in 1928 -29, and the top 100 MPs during the 1929 – 31 Parliament included Bondfield and Wilkinson. Reinforcing the view that women needed to be more vocal, Ellen Wilkinson stated in a debate on unemployment on 29 June 1925:

> "As I am the only woman Member of my party in the House, I must say something on this head." [6]

Professor Brian Harrison has undertaken a helpful analysis of the contributions by all the women MPs from 1919 – 1945 on welfare issues, noting that welfare is prominent in the debating profiles of them all, not just the Labour women . Even though Margaret Bondfield and Susan Lawrence spoke more on welfare than any other female MPs, most women MPs seemed to acquiesce in the remarkably male-dominated discussions on unemployment and welfare, possibly for the simple reason that since they were so few in number, the women MPs simply could not do everything. It is, though, perhaps surprising that the Labour women MPs were relatively reticent in the debates on the Beveridge Report in 1943 – 44 and the 1944 Education Bill, later to become the 1944 Education Act which transformed Britain's system of schooling.

There were, however, specific topics which related solely to women. Ellen Wilkinson and Edith Summerskill were both prolific speakers among the women MPs on equal pay, while it is Margaret Bondfield who unsurprisingly leads the field in terms of women's employment. Equal opportunity in the civil service was another "women's issue" championed by the Labour women MPs, which led to consideration of women's civil and military war service. Jennie Adamson and Edith Summerskill proved the leading advocates on these particular topics and the latter also pressed for greater representation of women on public bodies.

Yet the women MPs of all parties developed solidarity, including cross party friendships such as that between Ellen Wilkinson and Nancy Astor. Moreover, the women MPs of all parties were careful not to attack each other in public. When Nancy Astor was in full flow, attacking Labour for Britain's economic collapse, Astor refrained from singling out Bondfield, recognising that the Cabinet Minister was in an impossible position.

Survival as a women MP at this time required a bunker-like attitude, vital in a male orientated environment and made more necessary by the physical segregation of the sexes in Westminster, with the women MPs given their own, separate office. In 1924, Ellen Wilkinson together with the Conservative woman MP Nancy Astor and Mabel Phillipson, shared an extremely cramped office, unsurprisingly known as the "boudoir". Ellen herself describes it as:

> "Really rather like a tomb…Yet this was where much hard work had to be done. We should have something larger…Often we are in the House from ten

in the morning to midnight, with frequent all-night sittings…baths are provided or the men, but not for us." [7]

However, the women MPs soon began to want more space and to become part of the mainstream life in Westminster. The Labour women MPs campaigned to get women secretaries of ministers and opposition leaders admitted to the Strangers' Dining Room on the same terms as their male equivalents, finally triumphing in 1928. The *Daily News* could now claim that "great use is made of the smoking rooms, which were once dedicated to men." [8] The appointment of Lawrence, Wilkinson and Hamilton as parliamentary secretaries widened the frontier as they needed to keep up with smoking room gossip.

Ellen Wilkinson, ever full of energy, became a member of the House of Commons Kitchen Committee during the 1924 – 29 Parliament, with the aim of trying to improve accommodation and related matters for the women MPs. However, office provision remained woeful and, to add insult to injury, the women members had a difficult walk of about a quarter of a mile to the lavatory when a division was taking place. Even in 1929 when the fourteen women Members were allocated a new room they still had no bathroom. The prevailing attitude was purportedly summed up be one of the officials responsible for accommodation in the House of Commons, "They come here as Members, not as women, and are supposed to share everything with other Members" [9]

The question of what would become to be known as sexist language and behaviour was pursued vigorously by Edith Summerskill:

"I have been ladylike for too long…be quiet and try to behave like a gentleman," she declared when constantly interrupted during a debate recommending a National Health Service in 1945. [10]

When the MP John McGovern used the word 'manpower' in a debate on women's war service, Summerskill was quick to condemn the use of a male term when talking about women, while her trenchant views on the wartime poster with the slogan "be like Dad, keep Mum" were made very clear to the Ministry of Information.

In the run-up to the Second World War, the Labour women MPs found themselves discussing the rise of Hitler, specifically appeasement. In August 1930 Ellen Wilkinson came down mercilessly against appeasement, stating that Chamberlain was "putting the narrow interests of his class…and of the rich before the national interests." [11] Once at war, Westminster's political leaders formed a coalition government which had the effect of bringing the women backbenchers together. It would appear that the women MPs played some part in ousting Chamberlain, with Ellen Wilkinson taking a leading role. The war itself ushered in a climate of egalitarianism unknown during the 1920s and 1930s. The new-found spirit of equality assisted equal pay for war workers and equal compensation for bomb victims. Edith Summerskill, as ever, got to the nub of the matter when she asked the pensions minister to explain why a women's arm or leg is not of the same value as a man's [12]. Interestingly, during the war years women overtook men in their annual debating contribution in the House of Commons.

When the period 1918 to 1945 is taken as a whole, it becomes very clear that the Labour Party's changing electoral fortunes were central to the experience of its female MPs. In 1931 the formation of the National Government and the resulting splits on the left destroyed the careers, at least in the short term, of Bondfield, Hamilton, Lee, Manning, Phillips and Picton-Turbervill. There was, in fact, total wipeout in 1931 with every single one of the Labour women MPs losing her seat. Less traumatic election defeats saw off Bondfield, Lawrence and Jewson in 1924. While the first two returned in 1929, Dorothy Jewson was lost to Parliament all together. Ellen Wilkinson was again the only Labour woman MP elected in the general election of 1935 which saw the formation of the second National Government, though she was later joined by Edith Summerskill and Jennie Adamson, both returned in by-elections in 1938.

The first Labour women MPs lived precarious lives filled with hard work often in a less than satisfactory working environment. They had to put up with jibes, opprobrium and worse from many of their male colleagues, and gained precious little recognition for the contribution they made to public life. The fact that these tough and indomitable women pioneered women's representation in national politics in the United Kingdom seems to have by-passed the establishment both then and now. The names of all but the most well-known have sadly fallen out of our collective memory. Although Ellen Wilkinson has always been something of a star, Margaret Bondfield has almost disappeared from view, though thankfully she is re-emerging with the proposal to erect a blue plaque on the site of the shop where she worked in Hove, West Sussex.

Yet the most important point is that they were there. The Labour women MPs in the 1920s and 1930s had entered a man's house and succeeded there, publicly demonstrating that women could achieve in high profile and important work outside the home and that, given the chance, they were just as capable as men. All of them without exception contributed to the maintenance of parliamentary democracy during the upheavals of the 1930s and the subsequent years of conflict. They had been tried and they had succeeded.

Just as Ellen Wilkinson, from her election in 1924 until her untimely death soon after the 1945 Labour landslide, was the leading woman of her generation in the House of Commons, the equivalent within the ranks of the Labour Party was the Chief Woman Officer Dr Marion Phillips. MP for Sunderland from 1929 to 1931, Phillips will always be remembered for her ground-breaking work for women in the Labour Party as a whole. Appointed as Labour's Chief Woman Officer when women's sections were established following the adoption of completely new constitution for the Labour Party, she tirelessly recruited women to the Party and developed the women's organisation into a coherent body with a real role to play.

Marion Phillips, born in Melbourne, Australia in 1881, came to Britain in 1904

Marion Phillips at her desk in 1908

to study at the London School of Economics, and her initiation into the Labour movement came four years later working for Fabian pioneer who founded the LSE, Beatrice Webb. Phillips joined the Women's Labour League, the forerunner of the Labour Party women's sections, and never looked back, becoming its secretary in 1912. Unlike the leading suffragettes, Phillips's main political aim was not to extend the franchise; she not only wanted state interventions in the market, she also believed such interventions should be better informed by considerations of life outside the workplace, such as the experiences of working-class women and housewives.

Her early work editing the League's leaflet expanded greatly when it became the journal *The Labour Woman*. Between 1917 and 1932 Marion Phillips, indefatigable as ever, also worked as secretary of the Standing Joint Committee of Industrial Women's Organisations (SJC), an important meeting point for women from the Labour Party and the trade unions. She saw her role as keeping the Labour

Party informed of the needs of women and providing women with the means of becoming better educated in political matters. The Women's Labour League (WLL) was formed in 1906 and provided a forum whereby women could be involved in political life, and specifically the affairs of the Labour movement. It was absorbed into the Labour Party in 1918. Political in a way the Women's Co-operative Guild was unable to be, the WLL developed into an effective voice for Labour women. The League enabled women to see that they could have power as women and not just as wives and mothers.

In its early days under Margaret MacDonald, the WLL's greatest achievement was education and training. Discussions at its first meetings in the early 1900s often centred around women's own experiences – water supply, sanitary dustbins, flannelette and fireguards [13]. At the 1909 WLL conference held in Portsmouth, resolutions included the medical inspection of school children; poor law relief as a disqualification for the franchise; unemployment; state insurance for widows; votes for women; and state control of hospitals. The successful campaigns for votes for women and raising the school leaving age can be traced back to the early 1900s.

By 1908 the Women's Labour League had achieved enough status for two of its members, Katherine Bruce-Glasier and Mrs Simm, to be invited to an Independent Labour Party (ILP) Conference in Huddersfield. Notwithstanding the later fate of the ILP (which eventually withered away as the Labour Party gained in strength), the WLL's inclusion in the deliberations at this time was significant. The MP Fred Jowett, soon to become ILP Chairman, expressed his support for the Women's Labour League referring to:

> "…the splendid work of the League in stimulating the interest of women in Labour politics, in fitting them to do useful work on local governing bodies, and in training them to fight side by side with their men comrades at election times."

The Women's Labour League, under Marion Phillips's determined leadership, merged with the Labour Party in 1918 after the Party had reorganised its constitutional arrangements. WLL branches became women's sections of the fast growing and increasingly significant Labour Party. Having established the Labour Representation Committee in 1900 the Party had forty-two MPs at the outbreak of war in 1914. At the same time, the grassroots organisation expanded rapidly from 375,931 in 1900 to 1,612,147 by 1918. However, prior to 1918 these members could not join on an individual basis, but only through an affiliated trade union or a socialist society.

The creation of individual membership whereby anyone could join the Labour Party directly was the most significant change in the 1918 constitution. It was particularly important for women, most of whom did not work and therefore were not members of a trade union. As part of the process of building a mass party with popular appeal across the whole of British society, the Labour Party was beginning to realise that it needed the support and votes of women. Arthur Henderson, who with Sydney Webb was the principal author of the new constitution, aimed to use the revised structure to do just this, albeit reflecting the prevailing view across western society that men and women occupied separate spheres. The result was the creation of women's sections and four, later increased to five, seats on Labour's ruling National Executive Committee.

Work began on establishing women's sections immediately after the Labour Party Conference in 1918 had adopted the new constitution, and Marion Philips took up her position as Chief Woman Officer. Described by Beatrice Webb as having "an insolently critical attitude towards all persons and institutions" [14], Phillips nonetheless proved eminently suited to her new job. Her main task was to encourage women to join and to look after those who did. In this capacity Phillips helped to put issues such as equality for women in the workplace, school meals, clinics and play spaces for children, the fundamental value of mothering, and the need for better designed housing on the political agenda.

Marion Phillips was a woman of truly Herculean energy and commitment. During her early years in the Women's Labour League she would come to meetings carrying a secretary's kit and demonstrating how best to use a card index. But it was not all about process and administration. During the lockout of 1926, Marion Phillips raised more than £300,000 for the miners' wives and children. Sadly she died prematurely of stomach cancer at the age of fifty having spent less than a year as a Member of Parliament. Her legacy lives on and she will always be credited for turning the Labour Party women's sections into vibrant membership organisations providing help and support to Labour women across the country.

The Labour Woman, which remained the journal for Labour women, recorded the creation of the first women's sections in April of that year in Norwich, Ainsworth, Irchester, Leigh, Liverpool, Lutin, Rushden, St Helens, Wellingborough and Wigan. Elizabeth Andrews, appointed in Wales in 1919 as the fourth Labour Party Woman Organiser, tells how the women's section at Ton Tree, Rhondda started in 1918. There were twelve women present at the inaugural meeting, which was called with the help of the local trades council. The South Wales Miners' Federation was at that time agitating for shorter hours and higher wages. When discussing the matter the women felt the time was long overdue for something to be done to lighten the burden on the miner's wife. As a result Elizabeth Andrews wrote to the miners' conference expressing support for their demands and also asking that shorter hours for miners' wives be considered. The letter was subsequently read to the conference and reported to the press. [15]

The first Women's Day was celebrated on 9 June 1923. John Cape expressed the feelings of many attending the Durham Miners' Gala that year in a letter to the Labour Party Chief Woman Officer Marion Phillips:

> "The great shining feature of the Women's Gala was the expression of service and the hope of future power. I read in the faces of our older women

the grim determination to finish their days by...giving such energy and spirit as was left in them after thirty-five to forty-five years of hard struggles against severe industrial conditions, to bring peace and security by political power to the peoples of the world." [16]

Worthy though the women's sections were they were not decision making bodies. The idea of separate spheres, male public and female private, still very much held sway. The women's organisation at national, regional and local level was purely advisory and the seats on the Labour Party National Executive Committee (NEC) were elected by the Party's annual conference, chosen in other words by the block votes of the trade unions. Neither did Labour women see themselves as part of any wider feminist movement, though it does seem to have been the case that various male members of the Labour Party feared that this was indeed what was happening.

At every annual conference between 1919 and 1925 women members were warned against approaches from feminist organisations. In 1921 the NEC denied the non-militant suffragists (in the form of NUSEC) representation at Labour women's conferences, and in 1925 a resolution that would have forbidden Labour women to be members of the NUSEC was only narrowly defeated [17]. The Chief Woman Officer and future MP Marion Phillips took a very hard line asking Labour women in 1921 "to have nothing to do with those who come in the guise of friends and ask them to co-operate in regard to certain individual parts of the Labour Party's programme." [18]

There seems to have been a mutual distrust between the Labour Party and external women's organisations, specifically those viewing themselves as feminist. That Labour women focused instead on class is hardly surprising given that was the very essence of the Labour Party itself and women had joined the Labour Party as a political party not as a single issue group. Labour was the Party of the working class, especially the industrial working class, and did not particularly want to ally itself with what it viewed as middle-class women in the suffrage movement.

The Labour Party women's sections extended their reach across the country during the 1920s and 1930s, growing rapidly in solid Labour areas. Although the first official statistics of Labour Party individual membership were collected only in 1928, it is possible to estimate the numbers based in data from *The Labour Woman*. In 1921 there were about 60,000 women members, rising to 250,000 by 1925 [19]. As their numbers grew the women members, aware of the unequal distribution of power in the Party, began to seek ways of improving their position. Dorothy Jewson, one of the first three Labour women MPs elected in 1923, summed up the feeling when moving four resolutions to the 1928 National Conference of Labour Women. Jewson's resolutions called for:

1. the national conference of Labour women to only consist of delegates affiliated to the Labour Party;

2. the conference to last three days and discuss all matter affecting policy and organisation;

3. the conference to have the right to put three resolutions on the agenda of Labour's annual conference;

4. and women members of the NEC be elected by ballot at the national women's conference.

The demand that three resolutions go to annual conference and that the women's conference elect the NEC women's section members were agreed by the women's conference, but inevitably got no further.

In 1921 the Labour women's conference passed a resolution to amend the Party's constitution so that the women's seats on the National Executive Committee were elected by the National Conference of Labour Women. There were also attempts to increase the representation of women on elected bodies. Although these and other attempts to increase women's power were not successful, they did at least get the ball rolling, albeit only within the Labour Party women's organisation.

By the second half of the 1920s Labour women began to seriously focus on how to secure more women parliamentary candidates. One of the main obstacles to women putting themselves forward was money, or rather lack of it. Two options to address this were considered, one local and the other national. The local one, the Durham scheme, decided on a candidate locally, circulated this to women's sections and asked them to guarantee a certain sum per year for the constituency. However it was the national scheme that won the day, but one still funded by the women's sections. This was at least a start in thinking how to overcome the problem of financing a campaign, a problem which many women continue to face.

The Labour Party itself also debated women's place in the Party. Amendments to the constitution were adopted at its annual conference in 1929, the alterations being:

1. five instead of four members on the NEC;

2. the qualifying number for constituencies to send an additional woman delegate to Labour Party annual conference was raised from five hundred Party members in a constituency to two thousand five hundred;

3. a national membership card and an increase in the fee;

4. the definition of the status and functions of women's sections and their representation on divisional Labour Parties.

One possible reason why these changes got through the notoriously male-dominated Labour Party Conference in 1929 may have been that Susan Lawrence became the first woman Chairman of the Labour Party National Executive Committee that

Front cover of The Labour Woman, 1929

year. This was a huge achievement which delighted women members of the Labour Party. The news made the front cover of *The Labour Woman*, the news magazine for the Labour Party Women's Section.

None of these changes increased either the power or the standing of the women's organisation, and Labour women expressed their discontent at the women's conference in 1930, where a resolution that the Labour women's conference be recognised as an official gathering and its resolutions accepted by the Labour Party was carried. [20]

Yet the women's sections continued to go from strength to strength. Labour women in the north-west region began to consider the House of Commons as an option. Agnes Hamilton was elected for Blackburn in 1929, and there were five women parliamentary candidates in the 1935 general election – Mrs Gould (Hulme), Miss Bulley (Chester), Mrs Mercer (Birkenhead East), Mrs Kirkby (Darwen) and Dr Summerskill, later to win a seat in a by-election, in Bury. A similar pattern would emerge throughout the nine Labour Party regions across the country.

Annie Somers, an organiser in London during the inter-war period, shared how her job was initially focused on breaking down prejudice against the political organisation of women. Antagonism against a separate woman's organisation is a recurring theme in the history of women in the Labour Party. The work of Annie Somers and the London Labour Party Women's Advisory Committee quickly bore fruit. By the late 1920s there were vigorous women's sections in all but a few especially difficult constituencies based on Labour Party ward boundaries, typically about one fifth of a parliamentary constituency.

Women Labour Party members gained some success in London during the inter-war years. Labour first gained control of the London County Council in 1934 and in 1939 Labour's Miss E.M.Lowe became the first woman to hold the prestigious position of Chairman. Miss Lowe had, in fact, come up through the women's organisation in the London Labour Party, having been president of the West Bermondsey women's section since its inception, as well as representing the London Women's Advisory Committee on the Party's Regional Executive Committee for many years. Labour in London also selected women to go to Westminster. Susan Lawrence represented East Ham while the East Islington seat was held by both Ethel Bentham and Leah Manning during the 1930s.

While the Labour Party women's sections played an important role in training and developing women, the Labour Party also viewed them as fertile ground for recruiting new members and *The Labour Woman*, the Labour Party's official women's journal since 1918, concentrated much of its efforts on encouraging women's sections to recruit more members to the Party. "In 1933 we had 154,000 members, in 1934, 158,000, and in 1935 172,000. It is good to report this steady increase but we want more" declared Mary Sutherland, Chief Woman Officer at the time who also edited *The Labour Woman*, at a women's section conference of 1936." [21]

To achieve her goal, Sutherland produced a plan based on the premise that women's sections should move with the times and appeal more to the woman wage earner. At the same conference George Shepherd, the Labour Party National Agent, also stressed the need for new members. The Labour Party had polled 8,300,00 votes in the 1933 general election, a quarter of the total votes cast, but the Party's fortunes had improved only slightly despite the obvious disarray of the Conservative government since the election. The Labour Party lacked proper electoral organisation and there was never enough money to fund campaigns. The only way to solve these twin problems was, according to Mr Shepherd, to recruit more members to the Labour Party:

> "We are poor today not because present members do not give enough – many of them are giving too much – but because not enough people are giving. We shall continue so until we increase our membership and the number of pockets to provide the requisite yearly income." [22]

Shepherd continued in the same vein. In 1936 Labour Party membership was four hundred thousand. The NEC aimed to raise this to one million to increase party funds to fight the Conservatives who had spent £200,000 on posters alone during the last election campaign. While unwilling to give the women's organisation any meaningful place at the top table, the Labour Party viewed women as useful. The message that women were vital in building up the strength of the Party was continually reinforced. Elizabeth Andrews expressed it thus in *The Labour Woman*:

> "Will you help? Labour calls you. The success of the whole Labour Movement depends on the individual efforts of its members. Let 1932 be a record year for membership."

At a time when educational standards were relatively basic and women were not expected to work outside the home, it certainly appears that the grassroots members of the women's section got a great deal for their membership. Mrs Purves of Blyth's women's section put it like this in *The Labour Woman*:

> "I joined the women's section and gradually learned what Socialism stands for. I canvassed at elections and found that I took to this sort of work, the same as a duck takes to water. I have learned to love my work in the Labour Party until it has become a part of myself. Before I joined the Labour Party I was of a very shy, retiring nature and very house-proud. I am still house-proud, but with a difference. I have even done my washing on a Sunday night, so as to be able to attend a Conference or Summer School test on the Monday. I have learned that Labour women do not neglect their homes (as many people think), but that we work much better and happier than when we stayed at home, as we know we are working for the common good of all."

In the same issue of the journal F. Blackmore from Newton Abbott wrote:

> "The Section brought me into contact with women whose lives were similar to my own, who had the same cares and responsibilities to face, but whose philosophy of life, their ideals and aspiration, I came to admire, making many loyal and firm friendships in being associated with them."

Also in the same issue of *The Labour Woman*, Margaret Davis felt that:

> "It must be obvious to all 'thinking' women that everyone needs an outlet or means of escape from the hurly burly of everyday life...in my case I find association with the Labour Party women's section provides me with the fullest measure of self-expression...I find that it keeps one in close touch with all the difficulties and trials that confront the average working-class woman." [23]

The last word should come from the Chief Woman Officer Mary Sutherland in her editorial in the August 1936 edition of *The Labour Woman*:

> "It is the purpose of the Labour Party to replace that [the profit-making] system, which can only work through social inequality, and insecurity for ordinary folk, by a planned and ordered system based on human needs. That is why so many women have joined its ranks; that is why they find time from their busy and crowded days to carry on its work; that is why they make real and ungrudging sacrifices to provide pennies to keep its organisation going. Their common experience, their common conviction, and their common efforts bring the Labour women in every corner of the   country together in splendid fellowship."

Grassroots women clearly loved the women's sections, enjoying the company of like-minded women and solidarity with the Labour Party, but that was about as far as it went. The Labour Party's initial claim to offer support to women and integrate them into the Labour Party on the same terms as men had, quite simply, not become a reality. Neither the Labour Party's policies nor its organisational structures showed any great commitment towards the advancement of women within its ranks. The Party instead reproduced "gendered identities central to the culture of Labour" [24]. Most women were not happy with this; they wanted to be partners with their male comrades. The Labour Party of the 1920s and 30s was a long way from meeting this aspiration.

The Labour Party's structures, which gave power to the male dominated trade unions, worked against women gaining very much at all during the years before the Second World War and later. However, it has to be said that there were individual men in the Labour Party who were fully open to women gaining positions and becoming elected representatives. No less a person than Keir Hardie was certainly in favour of women's advancement. Yet there were those men who did not approve of women's independent tendencies, holding firmly to the dictum that a woman's place was in the home. While the problem obviously lay with individual attitudes

- and by extension a collective culture not only in the Labour Party but throughout society as a whole - a major issue was the way in which the Labour Party was structured after 1918.

The constitution adopted in that year reflected the importance of the trade union movement in shaping the Labour Party at its inception. In 1899 the Amalgamated Society of Railway Servants put a resolution to the Trades Union Congress to summon a special conference of trade unions, co-operative societies and socialist bodies to make plans for Labour representation in Parliament. The resolution was passed and arrangements made for the special conference held on the 27th and 28th February 1900 in Memorial Hall near Ludgate Circus in London. This conference established the Labour Representation Committee (LRC), the forerunner of the Labour Party. Thus, although it may not have seemed so at the time, the Labour Party was born. By 1903 at its conference in Newcastle the LRC was able to consolidate itself and tighten its constitution. This was thanks in part to a number of unions joining after the 1901 Taff Vale judgement in the House of Lords upheld the action brought by the Taff Vale Railway Company against striking members of the Railway Servants Union, ordering the union to pay both damages and the company's costs.

The Labour Party therefore started its life as an affiliate body made up largely of trade unions. Representing workers in heavy industry (where the majority of working men were employed in the early 1900s) it was inevitable that the organisation would be very heavily male dominated, a state of affairs made more acute because the only way into the LRC was via one of the affiliated male organisations. While some brave women, Margaret Bondfield being one, did come up through this structure it was the exception rather than the rule. Likewise Marion Phillips being nominated for the Sunderland parliamentary seat by the Monkwearmouth miners was a rare example of a woman being supported by male dominated trade union branches.

Thus, despite the opening up of Labour Party membership to individuals under the new 1918 constitution, the Labour Party's ruling National Executive Committee and the Labour Party annual conference remained dominated by the trade union block vote. There simply weren't enough women in the Labour Party to make any substantial difference to this state of affairs. It is, however, also true to say that there is no discernible evidence that women in labour movement organisations such as the Women's Labour League and the Co-operative Women's Guild in the 1900s challenged the way Labour representation was set. The notion of separate spheres reflected the realities of late Victorian and Edwardian society. Women may have noisily campaigned for the vote, and Labour women during the 1920s and 1930s most definitely wanted better conditions for those issues which affected them in their roles as wives, mothers and homemakers. However, they did not seem either able or willing to challenge the Labour Party constitution at the time and prevent it being set up to conform to the idea of separate spheres for men and women. [25]

Opposition came from both sexes in Britain during the 1920s. Some experienced women activists feared the women's sections would marginalise women members and their concerns, restricting women's role to one of organising social events. There were also men who just did not believe women could participate in collective action and wanted their wives to stay at home. Although Mary Sutherland, the Party's Chief Woman Officer, thought by the 1930s that hostility to women's sections was declining, she still felt the need to defend the sections against critics at the women's conference in 1946.

Although the women's sections were separate from what could be described as the Labour Party mainstream, they still very much saw it as their job to encourage and support women becoming elected representatives, a topic which occurs regularly in *The Labour Woman*. In 1927, as on other occasions, the national women's conference discussed proposals for increasing the number of women candidates, adopting a report on the matter with the following statement:

> "In view of the unanimous feeling of the Conference that it is in the interests of the Labour Party for facilities to be found for the adoption of more working (and especially married) women candidates, it is resolved that the National Executive shall be asked immediately to consider any means to that end"

Once they had attained a position, most of the women who succeeded at least kept in contact with the women's organisation, even though there were no formal channels for facilitating this. Ellen Wilkinson delivered the Chairman's address at the national women's conference in 1925, delivering a speech strongly critical of recent government proposals on widows' pensions which she considered to be inadequate and pointing out that they were far lower than those provided by the army. *The Labour Woman* was often used by the women MPs to communicate with women in the Party. Dorothy Jewson is quoted in January 1924 as saying:

> "Labour women must see to it that unemployment and housing are dealt with first because of the widespread misery and distress they are causing. The problem of unemployment amongst women has been a special one ever since the war period and has been disgracefully neglected by past governments... There are questions affecting the political and legal status of women on which I hope it will be possible for all women to unite...But more vital to women are all questions affecting the welfare of the child." [26]

A month later *The Labour Woman* reported on Susan Lawrence's maiden speech in the House of Commons and the journal carried regular contributions from her, mainly on children's issues and education. While the Labour women MPs, and most certainly those elected in 1923 and 1924, were quite assiduous in reporting on their work in the House of Commons, it was still the case that women attaining leading positions in the Labour Party differed from the activists in several respects. They were predominantly middle-class, well-educated and unmarried. Working-class and less educated women, the overwhelming target-group for the women's sections, remained under-represented and marginalised in the Labour Party decision-making process. As a result the women who actually got into positions to shape policy and who dominated the political discourse had very different life experiences from those shared by the women the policies were designed to support. Beatrice Webb was typically caustic about Susan Lawrence and this very problem:

> "In order to keep in touch with what she imagines to be the proletarian mind she has lost touch with the facts as they are…It is a bad case of the occupational disease so common among high-strung men and women who come out of a conservative environment into proletarian politics. By continuously talking to another class in the language they think that class speaks instead of in their own vernacular, they deceive themselves and create distrust in their audience." [36]

When the personal feeling is stripped away from Beatrice Webb's barbed and rather unpleasant view, it does highlight another issue always faced by elected representatives, namely that of translating the hopes, fears and endearing idealism of many members of a political party into something tangible in the body to which they have been elected. Labour women at the grassroots were passionate about making the world a better place for their families. It would, of course, have been utterly impossible to put the burden of realising their demands on the Labour women elected between 1918 and 1939. They were at the mercy of governments putting forward legislation and the Labour Party winning elections. The lack of women at the top table made it difficult to get the concerns raised by the women's sections into Labour Party election manifestos, and even if they were, the Party was only in government for a little over three years during 1918 – 45, discounting MacDonald's National Government. It is perhaps these particular circumstances which explain why the first Labour women have never received the recognition due to them.

They were also at the mercy of appalling economic conditions. The Great Depression would have defeated any government. As it was, Ramsay MacDonald's decision to form the National Government split the Labour Party and kept it out of power for a generation. As if this were not enough war loomed, ensuring that politics was far from business as usual during much of the 1930s. The early Labour women MPs did not have it easy, and their performance was undermined further by the volatility of the political environment. The late 1920s and 1930s were a difficult time for everyone. Against this backdrop we should perhaps be surprised at what was achieved by the Labour women during this period and by the first Labour women Members of the House of Commons.

References:

1.   Daily Herald, 30 October 1936

2.   Hansard 1936

3.   Fabian Quarterly, March 1947

4.   Jack Lawson MP, Methodist Magazine, April 1947

5.   Hansard 1928 and 1943

6.   Hansard 1925

7.   Liverpool Express, 28 April 1926

8.   G.Eden Daily News, 16 November 1928

9.   Jach Beiby in New Dawn 8 November 1924

10. Hansard 1945

11. Hansard 1939

12. Hansard 1941

13. *The Labour Woman* Feb 1933

14. Beatrice Webb, *Diary 3*, 302, 1918

15. Elizabeth Andrews, *A Woman's Work is Never Done*, 1952

16. *The Labour Woman*. June 1923

17. Pamela Graves, *The Labour Women: Women in British Working Class Politics 1918 – 1939*, 1994

18. Kathrin Ruhl, *The Influence of Women on the British Labour Party in the 1920s*, 2004

19. *The Year's Work of the Labour Party in Women's Interests at Home and Abroad*, June 1930

20. Mary Sutherland, address to the Business Conference of women's sections in 1936, cited in *Labour Women* May 1936

21. George Shepherd, *Wanted: A Million Members, Labour Woman* August 1936

22. Elizabeth Andrews, Labour Woman, January 1932

23. *The Labour Woman,* August 1936

24. David Howell, *MacDonald's Party: Labour Identities and Crisis 1922 - 1931*, 2002

25. June Hannam, *Women as Paid Organisers and Propagandists for the British Labour Party Between the Wars*, 2010

26. *The Labour Woman* January 1924

27. *The Diary of Beatrice Webb*, vol 4, 1924 – 43

Conclusion

Rt Hon Harriet Harman QC MP and Stella Creasy MP give their views on the way things are now

"As a woman parliamentarian you always have to pioneer." Harriet Harman, one of Labour's longest ever serving women MPs, is clear that things have not changed nearly enough. Furthermore she maintains vigorously that while there may now be more Labour women in the House of Commons, the power structures have not moved very far at all. Parliament is still dominated by men and run by and for them.

Harriet Harman first entered the House of Commons following a by-election in 1982 while seven months pregnant. There were two hundred and sixty-eight Labour MPs and three hundred and thirty-nine Tories. Harriet was one of only ten Labour women to be elected at this time, a statistic which tells the story as well as any words could. Shortly after her election, when just three per cent of the House of Commons were women, Harriet felt very strongly that something needed to be urgently done about the position of women in Parliament and about increasing women's representation. She therefore set about rallying the few women there and launched the first Parliamentary Labour Party Women's group.

Stella Creasy, on the other hand, joined the ranks of Labour women on the green benches in 2010, and therefore counts as a newcomer. "There are still more male MPs today than there have been women MPs ever," declares Stella Creasy before referring to Parliament as "Hogwarts gone wrong". Creasy claims the place itself is unwelcoming, referring to one occasion when she sat in "the wrong place" (there is no allocated seating for backbenchers in the Commons). MPs from a different party sat either side of her and talked over her, generally making it very clear that she was not welcome on that bench.

While there is an undoubted contrast between the early 1980s when Harriet arrived and Stella's debut in the early 2000s, in that by 2010 there were nearly one hundred Labour women MPs as opposed to ten when Harriet was elected in 1982, it is also clear that they have both faced similar issues in Parliament. The House of Commons remains a male institution with all that means for the ways in which power is exercised. Superficially Harriet's experience of being one out of ten Labour women in the House of Commons may seem much more like the situation faced by Margaret Bondfield, Ellen Wilkinson and Edith Summerskill. However, Stella and the new intake of women have also had to deal with entrenched male power and a fair degree of sexism.

Harriet Harman has always been a strong feminist and looked to women in the wider Labour Party during her time as an MP. "The Labour Party Women's Conferences were enormously important," states Harriet "because we had the women MPs, women Party members and women trade unionists. We all used to get together and plot what we would do." Harriet, together with like-minded Labour women, wanted to stand alongside the men. They envisaged the Labour Party women's organisation as the springboard which would ultimately deliver that.

Harriet Harman is, indeed, very clear about why she joined the Labour Party and later sought selection as an MP. "Labour is located in the right place to be the force for movement for women's equality and tackling inequality in relation to women as well as in relation to class." As the party of social justice, Labour was the natural political home for those wanting to improve the position of women across the board. Harriet states that the majority of those in the women's movement in the 1970s and 80s were on the left, and wanted to challenge all aspects of inequality. "We were strongly of the view that it was not just class and we believed that women wanted to speak for themselves rather than having men speak for them," is how Harriet describes her motivation.

To put this into context, Harriet feels that many in her mother's generation generally followed the social conventions of the time and thought that men, by virtue of their gender, were more authoritative and by implication 'right' more of the time than women. There was, in fact, a big transformational change between her mother's and her own generation. The women's movement of which Harriet was a part wanted public policy to move forward in tandem with this change in attitudes and behaviour. She was certain that being active in the Labour Party was the way to do this.

Stella Creasy also talks about the Labour Party being the party of social justice. She does, however, have a rather different take on feminism than Harriet. Twenty-five years younger than Harriet, Stella believes her parents' generation (including her father) was, and still is, much more alive to feminism than either her brothers or her partner. The problem is that her brothers and their generation believe we live in an equal society. There is a complacency about their view which Stella finds it hard to overcome. She feels there are still a lot of unconscious barriers faced by women when people think they "get it" but that is not really the case.

In support of her argument, Stella tells a story involving the Sun newspaper, one of whose male journalists had said it was outrageous for Stella to wear a vinyl skirt to meet the Prime Minister. The journalist suggested the MP was "bold" to wear such attire. However, Stella says that not only was the journalist being offensive, and interestingly there were many who agreed with Stella on that, but his comments also highlighted the still widely held view that politicians are white men of a certain age who wear suits. Stella does, of course, acknowledge that there has been forward motion and the current scenario is much better than the one which confronted Harriet when she first arrived in Parliament. She does, however, feel that it is nowhere near where it needs to be and that new challenges have evolved. We now have both the old inequalities and the old prejudices together with new forms of behaviours. Challenging unconscious bias and unconscious limitations is hard to deal with.

Harriet and Stella want change, long lasting change which is more than just incremental. Harriet says of her early days in the House of Commons that the Labour women MPs, supported by Labour women in the country, were a very small minority wanting very big change. Stella put it graphically: "I don't want to look my three year old niece in the eye and say 'we made some incremental change and I hope you're happy with that, love'. I want to know I've pushed as hard and worked as hard as I could and done everything we could possibly do. I feel a very strong sense of responsibility about how we make things happen and how we mobilise. Just being angry isn't actually going to enable me to look my niece in the eye and know that I took action."

Male hostility towards women MPs was raised by Harriet and Stella who both feel it in the House of Commons. Interestingly, in this area their experiences do seem different from the first Labour women MPs. There seemed to be little outright, tangible hostility towards the first Labour women MPs in the 1920s and 1930s. The feeling towards them was rather that they shouldn't be there, but since they were male MPs they should behave like gentlemen - although this did not stop them from trying to exclude women from debates and other House of Commons activities. This may have been because the women were a 'novelty' and since there were very few of them at any one time they were not perceived as a threat. More importantly perhaps, women as a group in the Labour Party, although they may have aspired to greater influence, were not really seeking power in the same way as Harriet's generation. Indeed, the Labour women in the House of Commons during the inter-war years were a well-behaved bunch who toed the Party line, while the women's organisation in the country had fairly limited goals regarding the Labour Party National Executive Committee and other Party positions. Moreover, male power was dominant and women were in no obvious position to challenge it.

However, fifty and seventy years later respectively, both Harriet and Stella have faced hostility from male MPs and men in the Labour Party, not to mention the media. Harriet experienced often quite nasty opposition from men in Parliament and the Labour Party, who thought the women's agenda was by implication attacking men and male politicians in particular. Male MPs thought Harriet and the women were saying that men were not able to represent female constituents and that they cared more about their male voters than the women. Too often the male response was defensive, that we (the men) are going to be critical of you because you are critical of us. As Harriet pointed out at the time, and has said over and over again since, she and her fellow feminists were not being critical of men individually but of a system which meant that Labour, the party of equality for all, was only effectively a party of equality for men.

Harriet maintains that while women remain in a small minority they will get squeezed out wherever there's a competition for power, unless the women have a real sense of what needs to be done for the sake of the party. Political power is a battle within parties as well as between them. No man was going to be prepared to give up his seat at the top table for a woman in order to further women's representation. Having said that, Neil Kinnock was keen to ensure there were more women in the Shadow Cabinet, and in 1989 it was agreed that three places in Labour's Shadow Cabinet should be reserved for women.

Harriet, who was a prime mover in bringing about this change, describes the level of male hostility it caused. Dubbed the "assisted places scheme" - a derogatory reference to a Conservative education policy whereby fee-paying schools allocated a few of their places to those coming from state schools - the new system did not benefit Harriet in that she did not get elected in the first round. There was, she said, a lot of anger and opposition from the men and she was being punished for arguing for it. Harriet was even accused of not being "clubbable". In actual fact she was unable to hang around Westminster as she had to get home to very young children.

Stella also talked about hostility of a different kind, but still clearly hostile behaviour. She tells of the time when she was attending a parliamentary committee as a shadow minister. Every time she spoke the minister kept saying she was emotional, irrational and other similar words. As if this was not bad enough the debate was about cyber-crime, something in which Stella is both very interested and well informed. Stella, however, stuck to her guns metaphorically speaking and did get some support from others attending the meeting.

Another issue which raised the hackles of many Labour Party men and women was the introduction of all women shortlists (AWS) when deciding on candidates for parliamentary seats. Selected some years before all women shortlists, Harriet is quite clear that when her constituency Labour Party chose her as their prospective MP they were very conscious that Labour could not be the party of equality while there were so few Labour women MPs. Harriet was, however, a leading campaigner to get the Labour Party to adopt all women shortlists, and describes how women in the Labour Party and the trade unions caucused to get issues concerning women though the Labour Party structure. In the end this was how all women shortlists were introduced. Women in the trade unions made sure the issue was included in composite resolutions at Labour Party Conference, and that the trade union vote was then cast in support.

Stella was, in fact, chosen from an all women shortlist, and as she says, she will "sing it from the rooftops". She further believes that AWS isn't about the candidates; it's about the environment in which you're operating. "It's nothing to do with the candidates themselves, and that's what drives me crazy when people talk about it" she states. "People say things like 'oh is this woman good enough' and I think, well that's not the point. The point is you're changing what the electorate thinks."

It is, of course, the case that the Labour Party is the only party in British politics which has introduced a system to make representation in the House of Commons more gender balanced. Britain is behind much of Europe in this regard where quotas are more established. The idea of enabling women's representation to grow and for women to break the glass ceiling is, however, taking root in other parts of British and European society. Progress has been made recently to improve the numbers of women on the boards of major companies, while there are now more female than male graduates from British universities.

Harriet though is right when she says that women are still not on the same terms as men in politics. Labour is significantly ahead of the other parties but still has a way to go. She is sure that the reality in other political parties is that they look at Labour and wish they could have as many women. Harriet then says, "And you know they could if they had all women shortlists, but they actually can't because they are not feminists like we are. To be a feminist is to challenge power and to want change. If you're a Conservative you want things to remain the same – the clue is in the name." Harriet is very clear when she says that while the Conservative motivation is to get women to vote for them, Labour wants women to elect the party so that we can make sure a Labour government delivers for women. These two approaches are very different.

While Labour wages its battle to secure more Labour women in Parliament, the other political parties, while maintaining they also wish to improve women's representation, actually take very little in the way of concrete action. Stella Creasy thinks many Conservative women and men are what she calls "plastic feminists". Stella maintains that "it's easy to be a plastic feminist and say yes, I believe everything should be equal, but as soon as it comes to doing anything about it they melt." Stella believes we have to be steel feminists. We have to say we will rebalance power, which means that those who had power before will inevitably feel affronted.

Stella maintains these differing attitudes towards women's equality and gender balance hinder alliances with women from other political parties. While the early Labour women MPs were close to Conservative and Liberal women, partly out of necessity in that they all shared office and other facilities, these alliances appear to no longer exist now that practical necessity is not the prime consideration. By the time Harriet was elected there were separate members rooms for Labour and Tory women MPs. The adversarial nature of British politics explains the need for these separate rooms, yet it does nothing to encourage cross party working.

Harriet believes strongly that women's equality, and the power that comes with it both in the House of Commons and the wider world, is a numbers game. Once a critical mass is achieved, the presence of women becomes normalised and women can go on to achieve in an atmosphere which is far less antipathetic than the one she encountered when she first arrived in the House of Commons. However, it's a long journey and as both Harriet and Stella point out, the old prejudices remain. The story of Stella's altercation with a Tory MP about taking a lift in the Palace of Westminster is relatively well-known. When she was still a new Member, Stella got into a lift with a sign outside reserving it for MPs. Stella was, in fact, with another woman who was not an MP. A Conservative Member then came striding into the lift and said to Stella 'you obviously can't read'. He then continued to a bemused looking Stella, 'this is a lift for MPs and disabled people and you're clearly neither'. The MP insisted Stella show him her badge, which she managed to do in spite of carrying an armful of papers. Eventually the MP apologised to Stella, but at the same time made it clear that he objected to the other non-MP woman being in the lift.

Stella has direct experience of women speaking in House of Commons meetings and being ignored. She calls it the language of control because often a man will later say exactly the same thing and be listened to. Women are still not acknowledged or heard in the same way as men. As a woman you cannot do the right thing. If you're a woman and vocal you're difficult, if you're a woman and not vocal you're a wallflower. Stella believes that the dynamic in Parliament is still not fair towards women.

Harriet also has stories of being taken for a secretary or a member of the catering staff when she first became an MP. Worse perhaps is her story about Michael Foot, who addressed the Labour Women's Conference in Buxton in the early 1980s as Labour Party Leader. Foot delivered a forty minute speech to the Women's Conference during which there was no mention at all of women. Harriet remembers, "We all sat there with our eyes glazed thinking 'is he going to mention women?' He did the whole speech, which was intellectually extraordinary, but it was like, er hello Michael, this is the women's conference, there are 300 women sitting here." A measure of how far things have come is that no Labour Leader these days would treat the Women's Conference in such a way.

The idea that leadership teams at national and regional level should be balanced has also taken hold in the Labour Party. Harriet herself pioneered the balanced team with Gordon Brown. Later on there was a sense that the Leadership in Scotland should include both men and women and, importantly, that Labour would be disadvantaged with an all-male leadership. Harriet also mentioned that there is now a strong women's organisation in the Labour and trade union movement in Scotland and that progress is also being made in Wales. Labour women such as Pat Glass, Julie Elliott, Bridget Phillipson and Sian Williams have been elected as MPs in Scotland, Wales and the north of England. Labour also has a female Leader in the House of Lords and the British Labour Members in the European Parliament are also led by a woman.

While it is undoubtedly the case that the Labour Party leadership is more gender conscious than when Harriet became an MP, the House of Commons still has some way to go. For example, there are still not enough female lavatories. One of the worst recent examples of anti-women prejudice was that of "posh totty beer". For some appalling reason one of the House of Commons bars decided to sell this beer with a picture on the pump of scantily clad woman. The matter was taken up by Labour MP Kate Green who then received a barrage of abuse from both male MPs and some Conservative women who claimed the beer's name and the under-dressed female image were just a joke. Both Harriet and Stella firmly believe that feminism and equality are about having both an equal voice and equal respect.

Yet there have been improvements. Harriet points out that the institution of Parliament has changed for the better. When she was first elected the rules were more like a gentlemen's club than a democratic body representing the views of men and women. The Speaker is now acutely aware of that and has insisted on having a woman Speaker's Chaplain because he wanted to break the glass ceiling. Furthermore, the idea of having a woman among the team of Speakers and Deputy Speakers is absolutely entrenched. Parliament is therefore changing. Harriet believes this is due to the fact that there is now a critical mass of women MPs, and because of this women are now entering the mainstream.

Having children as a woman MP is also now much more accepted. Although there is still a long way to go, a woman can now go through the division lobby with a little baby and no-one thinks anything of it. This was certainly not the case when Harriet was having her children. She was in fact reported under the "I spy strangers" rule when a male MP thought she had a baby under her coat, which was not the case at all. The view at that period was that motherhood was something women did while men were engaged in public activity. Harriet tells the story of the time when she was in Committee and one of her Labour colleagues stood up and said on a point of order, "Mr Chairman, I just wanted to announce that I've had a new son born." Harriet, of course, wondered what he was doing in the House of Commons while his wife was giving birth.

Thirty years later the father would be expected to be with his wife or partner and new-born baby at such a time. Harriet feels that things have come a long way since she had children, saying "When I was first around it was very, very awkward trying to combine fighting for your constituents, fighting for a Labour government and also having babies." She continued, "With more women in parliament having babies you have the equivalent of the playground, when all the mums hang around at the end of the school day and they chat to one another and share experiences. You need to share ideas and information but I had nobody to talk to and had to work it all out for myself." Harriet then added that no doubt she got a lot of it wrong.

Stella Creasy on the other hand does not have children. The fact that this has been used against her provides just one more example that the double standard is still alive and well. She tells of an instance when she had been talking about immigration and the demographic challenges we face and the Daily Mail turned it into "MP calls for middle class women to have more babies." Stella is certain that at no point did she say such a thing or anything resembling it. Nevertheless the Daily Mail made a point of referencing that Stella was unmarried and not a mother. She says of this, "It's very frustrating, because if you give into this then it wins as a frame of reference. I've always believed that you don't let your opponents determine the terms of trade." It is worth noting that none of the Labour women MPs during the inter-war years had children while they were in the House of Commons.

Whether or not there are specific "women's issues" was a matter of slight disagreement between Harriet and Stella. Harriet is of the view that we need people from all walks of life in the House of Commons – people with children, without children, people from the north, the south, old and young and from all ethnicities.

However, when she arrived the House of Commons was definitely unrepresentative. Now Harriet feels it's great to see so many women MPs and to be able to normalise the agenda on childcare, flexible leave, domestic violence. As soon as a woman used to talk about these kinds of issues previously there would be a sort of hubbub among the men talking to each other. Now such matters are as much a part of the political agenda as money supply and the transport infrastructure. Harriet also says that a lot of women come to her and say "as a woman you will understand that …" Harriet therefore feels that she is acting as a representative, that she is advocating on behalf of the women who speak to her as a woman. Stella, suggests that we may be going backwards by slipping into a view that because more women are coming into Parliament they'll talk about different things rather than bring a different perspective. Both these Labour women agree that men as well as women should be publically debating issues concerning family life. "Male politicians should be talking about family life as well. They'll probably bring a different set of experiences and a different set of ideas," Stella said.

Both Harriet and Stella talk about the inspiring women who went before them. Harriet pays a special debt of gratitude to Judith Hart and Barbara Castle who both supported her. While Harriet felt like a lone pioneer it was far worse for the women who came before her. Barbara Castle and Judith Hart did not even have the support of the women's movement in the Labour Party outside Parliament. Fearless trailblazers such as Margaret Bondfield were superhuman. Harriet says, "You don't have to be super human to be a woman MP, you can be an everyday woman. But the earlier women MPs really were super human."

Stella talks about her family and how she feels she is lucky to have supportive parents. As a head teacher her mother was a great role model and showed that women could succeed in leadership positions. She also pays tribute to the Labour Leader in the House of Lords, Jan Royall, who she believes is a truly inspirational woman. However, even Stella has to admit that the House of Commons can be intimidating, but says, "the point at which I don't think it being intimidating really matters is the point at which I'll walk away."

Concern about appearance and image is a far less important differentiation between men and women MPs, but one which can cause grief. Harriet says "In a way there's a broader question beyond politics about women and image and how much of our value has to be attached to what we look like and how much we want to look good or how much we can afford not to care about it." There are also issues like whether to dye our hair, have cosmetic surgery, whether we are too fat or too thin. Image is a problem in our society so it's not surprising that it transfers into the political agenda. Harriet, however, thinks image is an issue for older women who feel under pressure to look young as well as for young women who may not be taken seriously if they look a certain way: "If a younger woman is too glamourous then she is regarded as too pretty for her own good, not to be taken seriously and leered at" states Harriet, "and if not, she's dismissed as being frumpy." Harriet feels that ultimately you just have to do what you feel comfortable with.

As women get older they face further issues. The danger for older women is that unlike men, who are seen to accumulate experience, authority and wisdom, older women may often be dismissed as redundant. Older women therefore face the double whammy of both sexism and ageism. You emerge from one problem into another.

Stella talks about regularly being called a "girl" even though she is nearly forty. This kind of pre-conception makes it considerably harder to do your job. She also talks about her time as a local councillor, when sometimes she was the only women in the room and found that tough, as was the rumour that she became deputy mayor because she was sleeping with the council leader. Stella Creasy has become well known for her campaigning to stop abuse of women in this way, particularly on social media. She supported Caroline Criado Perez when she received threats of rape and other assaults on Twitter following the campaign to get a woman on British bank notes. Stella has also had her own share of dangerous abuse and the police have recommended that she come off Twitter. However, as a public figure Stella will not do that, comparing the police suggestion to saying that she should not walk down the street. What she would really like to see is a proper process for dealing with online abuse and ways of stopping it.

Despite their coming from different political generations, one gets a sense that both Harriet Harman and Stella Creasy have faced much in common as female Labour MPs and in their political lives. It is quite clear that the House of Commons still has some distance to travel before women are treated as equals to the men. Yet there has been progress and the increasing number of Labour women MPs created through all women shortlists is making a difference. This means that, as Harriet says "men and women in the Parliamentary Labour Party have to walk the talk – you can't just talk about equality, you have to practise it. The fact that we've got so many more women MPs and so many more women in the Shadow Cabinet than the Coalition have in the Cabinet is defining our sense of ourselves." Stella says of her own journey, "I'm determined we make progress. I don't want to be a role model or a martyr. I don't want to be perfect; I just want to be good."

And this is a perfectly reasonable ambition in an institution that Harriet observes as "having more women than ever before, yet the basic structure remains unchanged."

Index

About the Author

Mary Honeyball has been a Member of the European Parliament since 2000. She is Labour's spokesperson on women and is a member of the women's rights and gender equality committee in the European parliament, a position she has held for over 10 years.

Mary has a long record of activity in the Labour Party women's organisation, having been chair of the London Labour Party Women's Committee and Treasurer of Emily's List, which aims to get more Labour women into Parliament. She was a London Borough Councillor from 1978 to 1986. Mary read Modern History at Somerville College, Oxford University. She went on to have a distinguished career in the charity sector before entering politics full time.

Mary has been a prolific writer for political journals and newspapers, including Total Politics, Guardian Comment is Free, European Voice, European Reporter, New Statesman and Tribune. She frequently appears on radio and television including the Today Programme, Newsnight, Woman's Hour, The Politics Show, BBC London, and both Iain Dale's and Ken Livingstone's LBC Shows.

In addition, she runs the successful blog, The Honeyball Buzz.

Photo permissions

Reproduced courtesy of Getty Images:

A rare cartoon of Susan Lawrence pg 10; Margaret Bondfield, Britain's first women Cabinet Minister, 1930 pg 22; Margaret Bondfield with Prime Minister Ramsay MacDonald pg 28; Ellen Wilkinson at a Jarrow Marchers' Lunch pg 33; Dr Edith Summerskill with colleagues 1939 pg 58; Mary Agnes Hamilton 1931 pg 75; Leah Manning and her Conservative opponent Thelma Cazalet in the East Islington by-election 1931 pg 102; Jennie Lee the politician in 1937 pg 107; Ellen Wilkinson at home pg 120; Susan Lawrence demanding equal votes for women pg 126.

Reproduced courtesy of the Press Association:

Ellen Wilkinson, Labour MP for Middlesborough East, in 1925 with trade union colleagues pg xix; Margaret Bondfield campaigning in Northampton pg 26; Jennie Lee on a train in 1931 pg 45; Leah Manning and Ellen Wilkinson pg 82; Lady Cynthia Mosley MP with her sister at Cap D'Antibes August 1931 pg 108; Marion Phillips at her desk in 1908 pg 133.

The cover photo is also reproduced courtesy of the Press Association.

Reproduced courtesy of the People's History Museum:

1924 General Election Poster pg xviii; Dorothy Jewson when North East District Organiser for the National Federation of Women Workers pg xx; Margaret Bondfield age 14 when she began her apprenticeship pg 3; Margaret Bondfield at the Women's Labour League Conference in 1910 with Mary Middleton and Mary Macarthur pg 4; Margaret Bondfield with Ellen Wilkinson and colleagues in 1927 pg 27; Margaret Bondfield in 1924 pg 31; Marion Phillips on the beach in Scarborough 1920 pg 36; Agnes Hardie 1937 pg 40; Mrs. Adamson presiding at International Women's Committee, Paris, August 27th 1933 pg 41; Ethel Bentham 1931 pg 43; Mary Agnes Hamilton 1931 pg 46; Susan Lawrence at the Ministry of Health pg 49; Refugees from Franco pg 78; Leah Manning goes to Spain in support of the Republicans pg 81; Leah Manning VAD 1914 pg 97; Leah Manning, National Union of Teachers Jubilee President 1930 pg 100; Ellen Wilkinson at Ardwick Higher Grade School pg 110; Ellen Wilkinson as a toddler pg 120; Labour Women in the 1929 Parliament pg 123; Susan Lawrence campaigning in the rain pg 126; Labour Women's Conference 1936. Society was still divided into separate sphere for women and men pg 127; Dr Marion Phillips MP claims to have been the first woman MP to have invented a really convenient House of Commons uniform which she is wearing in this picture. It consists of a well-cut overall of thick crepe-de-chine lined with bright silk and buttons over her dress pg 129; Front cover of The Labour Woman, 1929 pg 138.

Urbane Publications is dedicated to
developing new author voices, and publishing
fiction and non-fiction that challenges, thrills and
fascinates. From page-turning novels to innovative
reference books, our goal is to publish what
YOU want to read.

Find out more at

urbanepublications.com